HOW TO CATCH SALMON!

By
Charles White

Illustrations by
Nelson Dewey

Fishing Notes

Fishing Notes

Canadian Cataloguing in Publication Data

White, Charles, 1925-
  How to catch salmon-basic fundamentals

ISBN 0-88792-005-5

1. Salmon-fishing. I. Title II. Series.

First Printing: January, 1971
Second Printing: October, 1971
Third Printing: June, 1972
Fourth Printing: July, 1973
Fifth Printing: April, 1974
Sixth Printing: February, 1976
Seventh Printing: April, 1977
Eighth Printing: June, 1978
Ninth Printing: February, 1980
Tenth Printing: May, 1981
Eleventh Printing: May, 1984
Twelfth Printing: February, 1990
Thirteenth Printing: June, 1993

HERITAGE HOUSE PUBLISHING COMPANY LTD.
#8-17921 - 55 Avenue, Surrey, B.C. V3S 6C4

Printed in Canada

How To Catch Salmon

Sportfishing for salmon has almost become a way of life in parts of Canada, particularly on the Pacific Coast and more recently the Great Lakes. Many sportsmen live for an opportunity to test wits with the wily coho and chinook. And for beginners there is nothing more exciting than that first hit as the reel sings and the line peels out from beneath your hand. Here, in this revised edition of Charlie White's *How To Catch Salmon,* are all the techniques newcomers will need to know in order to enjoy this ever more popular pastime.

Very Important

Do not go fishing without first studying the current *B.C. Tidal Waters Sport Fishing Guide,* published annually by the Federal Department of Fisheries and Oceans. It is available free at sporting goods stores, marinas and similar outlets. The Guide contains all current regulations governing sport fishing not only for salmon but also for halibut, rockfish, crabs, oysters and other species. Check carefully the sections on spot closures which were introduced to conserve chinook salmon and remember that size limits apply to all salmon.

Front Cover

The big ones don't all get away. Velma McCall from Vancouver, B.C., with a 48 pounder taken while fishing out of Langara Lodge in the Queen Charlotte Islands, a region becoming world famous for its trophy chinook.

Rick Bourne of Langara Lodge reports that Velma caught her fish on a cut-plug herring near Coho Point during July. In that area the fishing season extends from May to October for some of the world's best coho and chinook fishing.

CONTENTS

Great Lakes Section

INTRODUCTION

One thing we should make clear at the very beginning. There are no hard and fast rules about salmon fishing. Almost every rule has an exception. Salmon are the most ornery creatures on the face of the earth and cannot be depended upon to do any particular thing at any particular time.

There are however, many general rules which apply most of the time and which are followed by

the fishermen who catch most of the fish. In reading this book, please remember that the guide lines suggested will have notable and spectacular exceptions.

GREAT LAKES SECTION

With this printing we introduce a new section of salmon fishing the Great Lakes of Ontario. Written by Darryl Choronzey, an acknowledged local expert on the subject, it imparts new wisdom which will be of interest and use to fishermen in both regions. We hope that you will enjoy it.

ABOUT THE AUTHOR

Charles White has been a compulsive fisherman since the age of six. In 1951-52, he worked as a biologist and photographer for the Oregon Fish Commission. He fin-clipped fingerlings at hatcheries, tagged migrating adults, and followed them right to their spawning grounds.

He spent three summers as a charter fishing guide on Vancouver Island, where he gained a reputation for consistent success using only light tackle. (His parties averaged almost eight salmon per trip in 1958.)

Charlie's love of fish and marine life led him to conceive and develop the Undersea Gardens in Victoria in 1963. These unique underwater chambers allow the public to view marine life in a natural environment. Three Undersea Gardens are now in operation, one in Victoria, one at Newport, Oregon and one in California.

For several years Charlie has been teaching salmon fishing techniques to night school students in the Victoria area. He also appears regularly on radio and television.

Most recently he has been conducting a series of experiments using a special underwater TV camera to film salmon approaching and striking a lure. The results of these experiments have been shown to packed houses across Canada and the United States.

He lives on the waterfront near Sidney on Vancouver Island.

SPECIES OF SALMON

We will concern ourselves primarily with chinook (spring, king, tyee) and coho (silver, also known as blueback) salmon although there is also good fishing for pink (humpback) salmon in odd numbered years. (This fish has a two year life cycle and only the odd year has a sizable run. The even years have almost been wiped out.)

In recent years fishermen using Buzz-Bombs and similar lures have had success with chum (dog, keta) salmon in late season at river mouths. In addition, tens of thousands of sockeye are now taken on trolled lures by both commercial and sports fishermen.

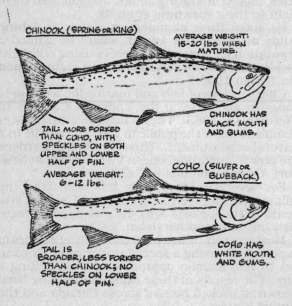

CHINOOK (SPRING OR KING)

AVERAGE WEIGHT: 15-20 lbs WHEN MATURE.

CHINOOK HAS BLACK MOUTH AND GUMS.

TAIL: MORE FORKED THAN COHO, WITH SPECKLES ON BOTH UPPER AND LOWER HALF OF FIN.

COHO (SILVER OR BLUEBACK)

AVERAGE WEIGHT: 6-12 lbs.

COHO HAS WHITE MOUTH AND GUMS.

TAIL IS BROADER, LESS FORKED THAN CHINOOK; NO SPECKLES ON LOWER HALF OF FIN.

DISTINGUISHING COHO AND CHINOOK

A coho can often be distinguished from a chinook by its tail (chinooks have spots and coho usually do not), but the most reliable method is to look in the mouth. A chinook has a black gum line (feeding chinooks are called "blackmouths" in Washington state), while it is almost white in a

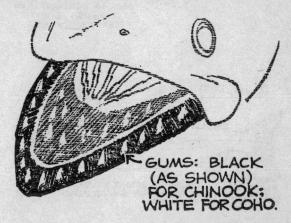

GUMS: BLACK (AS SHOWN) FOR CHINOOK; WHITE FOR COHO.

coho. Coho are a three year fish which average seven to ten pounds (at maturity). Chinooks mature at four years (some runs are five year fish) and average about 20 pounds, but can — and do — grow to 80 pounds and over.

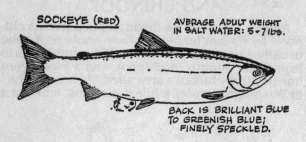

SOCKEYE (RED)

AVERAGE ADULT WEIGHT
IN SALT WATER: 5-7 lbs.

BACK IS BRILLIANT BLUE
TO GREENISH BLUE;
FINELY SPECKLED.

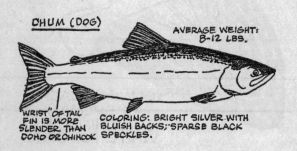

CHUM (DOG)

AVERAGE WEIGHT:
8-12 LBS.

"WRIST" OF TAIL
FIN IS MORE
SLENDER THAN
COHO OR CHINOOK.

COLORING: BRIGHT SILVER WITH
BLUISH BACKS; SPARSE BLACK
SPECKLES.

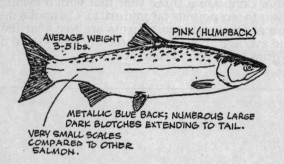

PINK (HUMPBACK)

AVERAGE WEIGHT
3-5 lbs.

METALLIC BLUE BACK; NUMEROUS LARGE
DARK BLOTCHES EXTENDING TO TAIL.

VERY SMALL SCALES
COMPARED TO OTHER
SALMON.

Jack Salmon

Many fishermen misuse the term "Jack" salmon. They incorrectly use it to describe any small salmon. A jack salmon is a male salmon which reaches sexual maturity earlier than normal.

Chinooks (usually a four year fish) have jacks which develop mature gonads in the second or

third year. These fish develop the normal characteristics of a full-sized spawning fish — darkening color, hooked over snout — at this time. Jack coho are only two years old (coho are normally a three year cycle) and are seldom over 15 inches or so in length.

Small chinooks caught by sports fishermen are usually immature feeding salmon of both sexes and not jacks at all.

EQUIPMENT

Tackle box

All plastic (to prevent rust) with large compartments in shelves. Many tackle boxes have small compartments designed for freshwater lures, but these have little value for the larger saltwater gear.

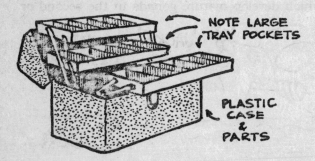

NOTE LARGE TRAY POCKETS

PLASTIC CASE & PARTS

It is not necessary to have a place to store a reel in the tackle box. I have yet to meet a salmon fisherman who regularly takes his reel from the rod.

Rod

I prefer a long rod (7 1/2 - 10 feet) with a sturdy butt and a springy tip. This is a good all-round rod, solid enough for handling a big chinook, but springy enough to give good sport on a small coho. I also like a long butt so I can rest it against my body when playing a fish.

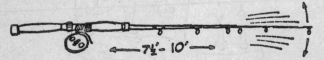

← 7½' - 10' →

The limber tip also acts as a shock-absorber when the fish runs suddenly.

If you plan to do a lot of deep fishing using wire line or planers, a short stiff rod is advisable.

Reel

There are three basic types:

Single Action: These reels are simply a plastic, wooden or metal spool with knobs mounted on a central post. A wing-nut or other screw adjustment allows you to adjust the tension. A ratchet provides that delightful screeching sound when a fish pulls at the line.

These have the advantages of simplicity, ease of maintenance, and (most important) they allow you to "feel" the fish, to play him actively by alternately winding and braking as the salmon runs and fights.

Some claim that they have a basic disadvantage in that you can't wind fast enough to keep up with

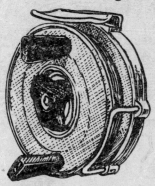

a big chinook running toward the boat, but I have never lost a fish for this reason. You also have to release the handles quickly when the fish runs or the line might break.

The handles can also be jerked from your hand and they will spin around hard, cracking you on the hand or fingers. This is why these reels are often called "knuckle-dusters".

My three boys have played salmon up to 40 pounds on these reels since they were 8 years old; so the problems of these reels are not serious.

Star Drag Multiplying Reels: These metal reels feature gear action which "multiplies" your winding action three or four times and has an adjustable drag which "slips" when the fish runs. These reels allow you to bring line in faster, and you don't have to release the handle when the fish runs since the spool slips automatically.

This "slipping" feature is to me the biggest

drawback of this type of reel. You can actually be winding in while the line is running out with a fish. You have no "feel" of the fish as with the "knuckle-duster", and much of the excitement is

lost. (If ease and convenience of getting the fish is your main concern, you could buy them in the fish market. It's much cheaper that way.) These reels are much more prone to corrosion or "gumming up", especially the level-wind mechanism.

Many beginners are tempted to tighten the drag to help land a stubborn fish, and many fish are lost when they make a last desperate run and break the line against the tight drag. (One top salmon guide has called these reels, "The best conservation measure ever invented.").

However, many experts swear by them and say they are the only kind for a real expert.

Spinning Reels: These are great for casting from the shore and from a boat. Get a heavy-duty salt-water model and keep it clean and well oiled.

When I first switched from trout to salmon fishing, my freshwater spinning reel was worn out after one season. The gears were ground smooth from the repeated long runs of big coho hooked on light tackle.

Spinning reels are used more and more as drift fishing becomes more popular. With this technique, a lure is cast from a drifting boat and "worked" back in, using a special technique described later in the book.

The Vital Link

When attaching reel to rod, many anglers use adhesive tape or plastic electrician's tape to hold the reel adjusting-ring in place. Usually these rings hold a reel snugly on the rod, but some tend to back off and loosen at critical moments.

When playing a big fish, the reel gets a lot of pulling and twisting which will sometimes loosen the locking ring. The reel could then slip completely out of the reel seat, leaving the angler with a loose reel and no way to control a hard running fish.

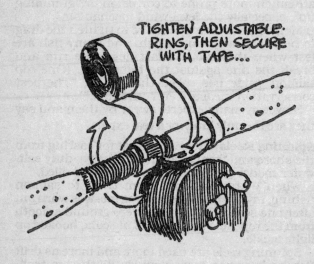

TIGHTEN ADJUSTABLE RING, THEN SECURE WITH TAPE...

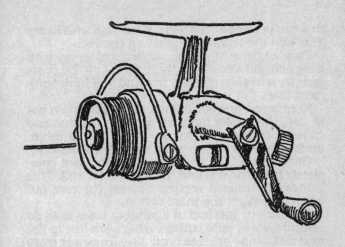

Line

Get plenty of line. I like 900 to 1500 feet of 20 pound monofilament nylon on my reels. I usually do not bother with any backing material although

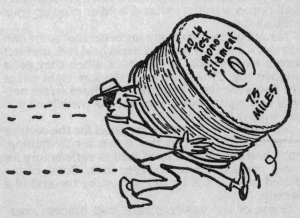

this can provide a "cushion" if you fish with heavy gear and the nylon is "tight" on the reel.

This length of line provides plenty of leeway with a big fish and also allows you to break off five or six feet (for a fresh end) each trip and still have sufficient line.

Keep nylon line out of direct sunlight when not in use. Ultraviolet light will weaken the line and cause it to become opaque. Store it in a cabin, under the gunwale or cover it with a piece of cloth.

Once a year, the line should be stripped completely from the reel and turned end for end. This brings the unused section nearest the core out where it will get the most action.

An efficient method of changing lines is to do several reels at once, transferring each line to the next reel. If one line has been used for two or more years, it can be stripped and discarded, leaving an empty reel on which to begin the line transfer.

Rod Holders

By all means, get a good set of rod holders. Nothing marks a fisherman as a rank amateur more than a boat with no rod holders. You can't troll properly trying to hand-hold or prop up your rods all day.

Many experts also share my belief that some fish are lost when they strike a hand held rod. Instinct forces most people to jerk back when they get a sudden tug. This often pulls the lure right out of the fish's mouth. They will sometimes strike natural bait again, but one chance is usually all you get with flies or spoons.

Adjustable rod holders are good for the serious fisherman (to get rod tips down for fly fishing, etc.), but the normal fixed unit is satisfactory for most uses. Get a top-quality unit. Some of the plated models will be full of rust by the end of a season.

Some of the newer plastic rod holders over-

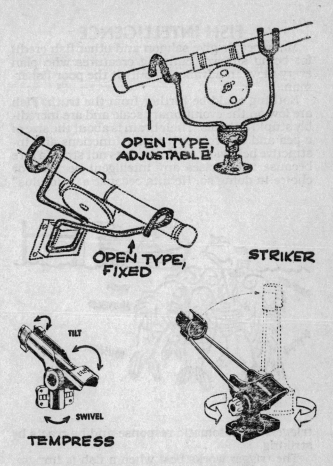

OPEN TYPE, ADJUSTABLE

OPEN TYPE, FIXED

STRIKER

TILT

SWIVEL

TEMPRESS

come the rust problem and have a wide range of adjustments. The "Striker" by Scotty and "Fish-On" from Tempress are two of the most popular.

FISH INTELLIGENCE

Many people give salmon and other fish credit for being shrewd, cunning creatures who plan every move in advance to outwit the poor fisherman.

Nothing could be further from the truth. Fish are low on the evolutionary scale and are incredibly stupid animals. Their brain is about the size of a pea and controls only motor functions and instinctive behavior. A salmon does not strike a lure because it exercises any intelligent decision or choice in doing so. He hits because a "stimulus"

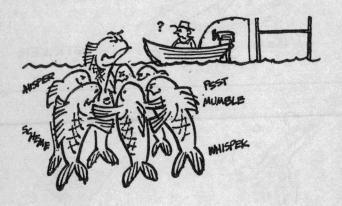

triggers an automatic response and he reacts by striking.

The trigger works best when a fish is hungry, specifically at certain feeding times. (Mature salmon at river mouths seem to strike a lure out of anger or irritation rather than a desire to feed, but no one knows for sure just why they strike at this time.)

The most effective trigger for a feeding fish seems to be a lure or bait which imitates a

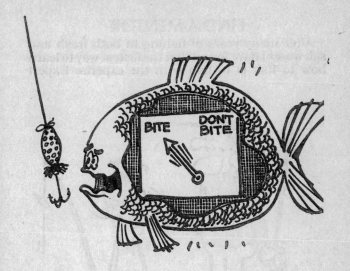

wounded herring or other bait. This erratic or wounded fish action is more important in triggering the strike than the detailed appearance of the lure itself.

This explains why salmon will sometimes strike at a plug, flatfish or other strange looking lure with hooks hanging all over it. (If fish had any real intelligence, they could never be fooled into taking such unnatural looking lures.)

Experiments with our underwater camera show that, while fish will take unnatural looking lures, they prefer natural lure imitations if given a choice. We are in the process of developing some new generation lures using photographic images to produce lures that look "picture perfect".

FIND A MENTOR

After many years of fishing in both fresh and salt water I have found that the fastest way to learn how to fish is to fish with the experts. Expert

fishermen are generally glad to share their knowledge with a keen fisherman who really wants to learn.

Each of the many experts who taught me about salmon, trout, bass, and even sunfish, catfish and carp had different theories and techniques for catching more fish than the next man.

I discovered however, that they all had one thing in common: *they were all very finicky about the lure itself.* They took great care in preparation. They also studied the lure carefully in the water.

making sure the action was right.

In trolling, this means watching the lure beside the boat and getting it exactly right before letting out the line. Next to knowing how and where to find the fish, being a perfectionist about lures is the most important secret of a top fisherman. If the lure or bait isn't right, nothing else matters.

You can have the fanciest equipment in the world, fish where there are plenty of salmon, but your luck will be poor if the lure doesn't trigger that instinctive reaction to strike.

PREPARING THE LURE

Sharpen the hooks

,A salmon slashing at a moving bait may only brush against the hook or the point will strike against a hard bony part of his mouth. A really sharp hook will catch or dig in where anything less will slip off and the fish is gone, in many instances without you even realizing you had a strike.

Hooks should be "sticky sharp". A good way to test this is to touch, lightly, the point of a hook on the centre of your fingernail. The hook should stick on this hard surface. If it slips to the side, the hcok is not sharp enough.

The importance of sharp hooks has been driven home to me by some exciting new experiments I have been conducting. Securing a special underwater television camera ahead of my lure, I can watch salmon attack the lure on a screen inside the boat.

It is amazing to watch one salmon after another nip lightly at the lure and swim away without being hooked. Some don't touch the hook, but others get it in their mouth and spit it out in a split second with very little disturbance to the lure.

Most anglers are probably losing more than half their salmon before they are even hooked!

I find it cumbersome to be continually sharpening hooks, especially when working three lines, and changing lures regularly. To solve this problem, I have developed an electric hook sharpener, operated by tiny penlight batteries. It puts a "sticky sharp" point on a hook in a few seconds, with no fuss or bother. It is available from many retail outlets or from Charlie White Productions, Box 2003, Sidney, B.C., V8L 3S3 for $21.95 plus $4.00 handling.

Prepare a good looking lure

Give your lure all the attraction possibilities built into it by the manufacturer. Shine metal spoons so that they have a glint and flash.

Be careful not to knock the scales off herring strips or whole bait fish. Be particularly careful when handling frozen herring or minnows that you do not break off pieces of the tail or fins.

Keep bait fresh in an insulated box with an artificial ice pack. Thaw a few pieces at a time in sea water.

When using plastic bait holders be sure you

follow the instructions and insert bait properly into the bait holder. Check the swivels on any type of spinning or revolving lures. Make sure that small chunks of dried seaweed or other obstructions will not prevent free action.

Check your line

It is good practice to break off four or five feet at the end of your line before you start fishing. This gets rid of any small nicks or scratches which might weaken the line.

Knots

There are a number of knots used in fishing, but the most popular on monofilament line is the jam or cinch knot. As much as ninety per cent of all knots tied in monofilament are of this type. It is ideal for tying lure to line, line to swivel, flasher to line, etc. Rhys Davis, inventor of the famous "Strip Teaser" lures, did some experiments with this widely used knot. There are a number of variations used by salmon anglers and Rhys tested their relative strength. He was amazed to discover that one version of the knot was far stronger than the others. Some very minor variations were sometimes only half the strength of the proper knot.

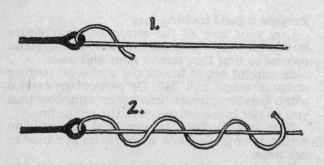

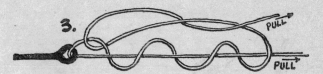

3.

PULL

PULL

WHEN KNOT IS THIS FAR ALONG, BEGIN PULLING
AT ENDS OF LINE. SLIDE LOOPS TOWARD EYE
OF HOOK AS YOU PULL KNOT SNUG.

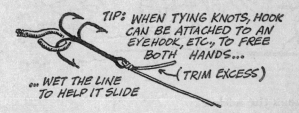

TIP: WHEN TYING KNOTS, HOOK
CAN BE ATTACHED TO AN
EYEHOOK, ETC., TO FREE
BOTH HANDS...

... WET THE LINE
TO HELP IT SLIDE

← (TRIM EXCESS)

Here is another variation, this one popularized
by fishing pioneer Rex Field. It's been called the
"Buzz Bomb knot" and works equally as well as the
one described above.

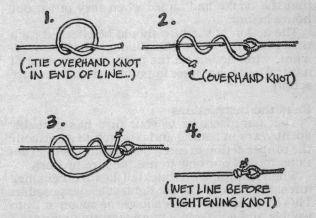

1.

(...TIE OVERHAND KNOT
IN END OF LINE...)

2.

(OVERHAND KNOT)

3.

4.

(WET LINE BEFORE
TIGHTENING KNOT)

Check the action

Here is a major area where most fishermen fall down. I have watched many so called good fishermen throw their lure into the water and start stripping out line without ever looking at the action of the lure in the water.

They will drag it around for hours only to find that the hooks had fouled when they put it out hours before.

The action of the lure should be checked each time you bring in the line. Changes in tidal movement, wind action on the boat, the softening of natural baits can cause important changes in lure action.

Read the instructions

The manufacturer of your lure has probably spent years in testing and research to get exactly the proper action to catch fish. Study his instructions to find out how to use the lure properly.

When using spoons, bucktail flies or other small lures, it is wise to use the lightest leader possible. This light flexible leader allows the spoon or fly to wobble and wiggle in a more tempting manner.

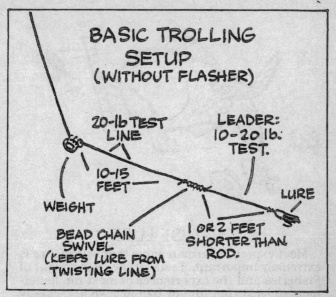

BASIC TROLLING SETUP (WITHOUT FLASHER)

20-lb TEST LINE

LEADER: 10-20 lb. TEST.

10-15 FEET

WEIGHT

LURE

BEAD CHAIN SWIVEL (KEEPS LURE FROM TWISTING LINE)

1 OR 2 FEET SHORTER THAN ROD.

New lure designs from underwater research

After 20 years of research with a remotely controlled underwater television camera, we have identified a number of strike "triggers" which appear to motivate all predatory game fish to strike under certain conditions. These strike triggers are:

1. The lure body should resemble a bait fish, preferably the bait on which the fish are feeding.
2. A wounded fish action. We found that a rolling, gasping, tight roll was most effective.
3. A sonic vibration like that of a small spinner attracted fish.
4. The tail end of the lure should be forked like that of a bait fish.

As mentioned, we believe that a detailed minnow-like appearance is also important. We have tested these new designs and results are very encouraging.

SIZE OF LURE

Most expert fishermen agree that size of lure is extremely important. Tests by the Department of Fisheries and the experiences of most top fishermen suggest that lure or bait size should closely match the natural feed in the area at the time you are fishing. If you can see some feed jumping or in the mouths of diving birds or in the stomach of a fish you have caught, by all means match this size.

If you have no clues, you might go by certain general guide lines. In late spring, summer and fall you will find candle fish in shallow areas with sandy bottoms.

There are often shrimp, squid, and small herring available in the summer and fall months. These suggest the use of a smaller lure such as a small spoon, minnows, or bucktail flies or flashtails.

In winter, large adult herring are moving through protected waters to their spawning areas and larger lures are more successful.

Of course there are always exceptions to these rules. The most important thing to know is the size of the feed in the area you are fishing.

FISHERIES DEPARTMENT DATA

The Canadian Department of Fisheries and Oceans performed some interesting experiments trolling with artificial lures off the west coast of Vancouver Island. With regard to lure size, the experiment indicated the following:

● Small spoons (under five inches) were far more effective for coho than large spoons or plugs of any size.

● Chinook salmon preferred large spoons which caught almost twice as many as large plugs.

● The study definitely indicated that large lures catch larger fish. Chinook salmon preferred large spoons and large plugs. The fish caught on the larger lures were much larger fish on average.

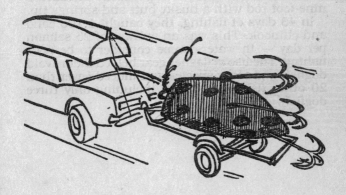

In Washington state, biologists ran a three month experiment to determine how many salmon could be caught by efficient anglers. They used four rods in one boat and fished in areas thought by many to be "fished out".

They used rotating flasher gear because it was

thought to be the most effective sport gear available. Tackle used in the experiment included a nine-foot rod with a husky butt and springy tip.

In 43 days of fishing, they caught 1,100 coho and chinook. This was an average of 25 salmon per day — in waters some consider to be poor fishing. The use of flasher gear helped them avoid dogfish and other species and indeed fewer than 20 other fish were taken, including only three dogfish.

COLOUR OF LURE

Fish seem to have color preferences, but they can change hour by hour. You must keep experimenting when using plugs or flies.

Natural Bait

This should be kept bright and shiny without disturbing the scales. If you are using a plastic strip teaser head, try one clear and one of the phosphorescent green. (My own preference is to use the green head when fishing deep and the clear head when fishing shallow).

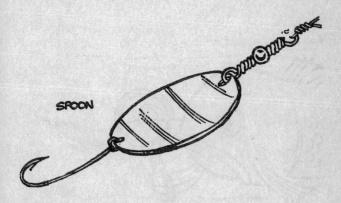

SPOON

Spoons, Wobblers

A spoon which reflects light seems to work best but abalone and mother of pearl spoons can also be quite effective. Some people use a spoon with red on it for pink (humpback) salmon and orange and black lures for spawning coho.

Hoochies, Flashtails, Bucktails

Color preferences are widely varied and sometimes the salmon are extremely fussy about tiny changes or shades of color. We have often trolled three apparently identical bucktail flies and have caught all our fish (sometimes five or six or more) on only one fly. There is some slight difference which triggers the strike on that fly only.

When coho are feeding actively, I have trolled a fly right beside the boat and watched the fish take it. They will usually dart up and study it closely with their eye only a few inches from the fly. Then they often drop back momentarily and come up on the opposite side to study it with the other eye.

Only then will they grab it and run. Other times they will just swim off without touching it.

So, apparently, salmon can distinguish fine nuances of color. I remember catching one coho after another on a grey ghost fly one morning when other grey ghosts were catching nothing but weeds. Examining it very closely, I noticed a very slight pink tinge to a few of the hairs.

I put out a pale pink fly and had a strike in less than a minute. The coho were looking for pink and had picked out the touch of pink in my grey ghost. One general tip is to try pink, ginger or red flies in the spring and fall when the shrimp feed is plentiful in many areas. (See Heritage House book, *Bucktails and Hoochies*, for complete details on colour selection and effectiveness.

If you are driftfishing, salmon can be color selective on Buzz Bombs, Stingsildas, etc. In late season, they often like darker colors, such as charcoal or dull grey. Sometimes they prefer a completely black lure. Many anglers are adding reflective tape to their lures. This tape is pressure sensitive and, after removal of the protective backing, is simply pressed against the lure surface. I have seen it used on spoons, plugs, spinners, Strip Teaser heads, and even on Buzz Bombs. This tape breaks up light into its component colors. Twisting and turning in the water, it reflects every color in the rainbow: red, orange, yellow, green, blue, and purple.

We don't really know how water coloration,

depth, or other factors affect what the *fish* sees. What may look red to us may look blue or black to a salmon under water. These reflective tapes (or the Twinkle Skirts described later) may increase our chances of success by giving the fish a flash of the color he is seeking.

EFFECTS OF LIGHT
ON THE WATER

Most experienced fishermen have observed that salmon are not at the surface when the sun is shining brightly on the water. They seem to bite best at dawn and dusk and sometimes on cloudy or rainy days.

There are many theories on why this appears to be true. One of the most interesting holds that salmon and other fish have no eyelids to shut out the bright sun. The iris in their eyes is also fixed and will not adjust to changes in light. This means that the only way they can escape bright light is to go down deep where light rays are diffused and filtered by the water. This explains why trout and bass fishermen find their best fishing on bright days under an overhanging tree or bank where the

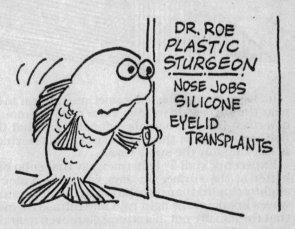

fish can lie in the shade. Perch and shiners are almost always found under docks, piers and other places where they can get out of the sun.

Following this same line of reasoning, it makes sense to fish for salmon in areas where the sun has not yet hit the water. This means fishing along the shaded cliff or tree-lined shore that blocks the early morning or late evening sun. It also means adding more lead and going deeper as the sun climbs and bears down more directly on the water.

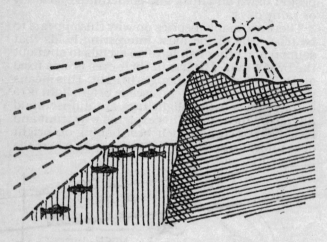

It also explains why fish sometimes appear to be near the surface, in muddy water near the mouth of a river. (What is actually happening is that the fish are just under the muddy layer of water which is filtering out the sun's rays.)

Expert bucktail fly fishermen say that coho bite better at the surface on days when the water is slightly rippled than on calm days. The ripples and waves break up the light rays and diffuse them so that the fish are not in a strong glare even near the surface.

POLARIZED SUNGLASSES

Sunglasses with polarized lenses are a great help in seeing through the surface glare on bright water. You can see the minnows and other feed far more clearly.

Most fisheries biologists wear them as standard equipment to improve vision on spawning streams and at sea.

FLASHERS AND DODGERS

There is a great deal of argument among fishermen about the use of flashers and dodgers. There is no doubt that they take a lot of the sport out of playing a fish because of the drag they create. There is also no doubt that they are extremely effective at certain times.

Flashers and dodgers are a help to inexperienced fishermen because they give an erratic action to the lure, especially when using a short leader between flasher and bait.

Even experienced fishermen find flashers and dodgers helpful. Recent experiments by the Washington State Department of Fisheries showed that the most effective and consistent lure used in their entire three month experiment

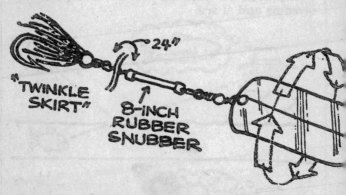

"TWINKLE SKIRT"

←→ 24"

8-INCH RUBBER SNUBBER

was a large revolving flasher and a lure called a Twinkle Skirt (a hoochy type of lure with clear plastic strips). This was deep fishing with 20 ounces of weight and wire line.

When fishing with flashers or dodgers, use a sturdy nine foot rod with a flexible tip so you can see the flasher action. Fish at the slowest speed that the flasher will rotate.

It is important to match lure to flasher or dodger. If the lure is too heavy for the flasher, it will dampen its action.

There are many arguments on the proper leader distance between flasher and lure. Most flasher manufacturers have recommendations on the package as to proper length under various conditions.

Generally speaking, the following guidelines should be helpful:

Leader length

The leader should cause the lure to dart sideways about an inch or so on each revolution of the flasher. Too short a leader will cause wide side jumps which make the lure hard for the fish to catch. Too long a leader absorbs the action of the

ROTATING FLASHER

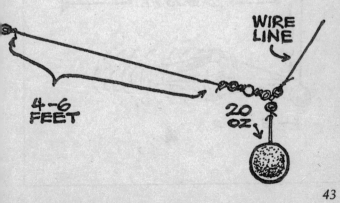

WIRE LINE

4-6 FEET

20 OZ

An Alternative Method

I have a strong dislike for playing a fish while dragging a flasher, but I do like the benefit of its fish-attracting features. Bearing this in mind I have been experimenting with a flasher on a downrigger, not attached to the fishing line.

The flasher is tied to a five-foot length of heavy nylon which is connected through a bead chain swivel to the swivel above the downrigger weight. The flasher rotates at the end of this line, but has no lure behind it.

The flasher works well on the downrigger wire, rolling over and giving off an attracting flash. Surprisingly, the rolling action also imparts a jerk or "beat" to the fishing line, adding an extra little darting action to the lure itself. This is true even with a 10-pound cannonball on the downrigger.

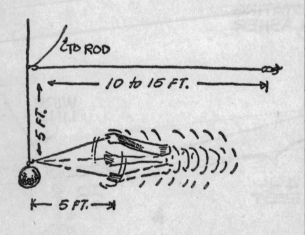

flasher and the lure has no erratic side darting action.

Coho like more action than chinooks, so leaders should be shorter when fishing for them.

Adjusting flashers

A dodger should swing from side to side in as large an arc as possible without flipping all the way over. This creates an attracting glint over a wide angle and also imparts the maximum erratic action to the lure behind it.

A flasher, on the other hand, is most effective when fished at the slowest speed at which it will revolve in a complete circle.

Flashers are usually trolled faster than dodgers.

The speed is right when the flasher rotates at the slowest uniform speed.

Some officials recommend that wire lines be used for flasher fishing. This is essential, they claim, because the stretch of nylon line distorts the smooth "beat" of the flasher being transmitted to the rod tip.

This rhythmic action of the rod tip tells you that the flasher is working properly. Any fouling of the tackle or even a small grilse will immediately change the action, allowing you to see and correct the problem.

When fishing several different lines, it is often difficult to get all your lures and flashers working at the same boat speed. Therefore, it is often necessary to adjust your flasher or dodger to make it work at a given speed.

If you want more action in your flasher or dodger, you increase the bend 1/3 from the end toward the lure. To reduce the action, increase the bend at the point about 1/3 from the end toward the line.

TO LURE

INCREASE THE BEND HERE TO INCREASE THE ACTION

TO ROD

BEND DOWN HERE TO DECREASE ACTION

BECOME A SPECIALIST

There are many different ways to fish for salmon and there are hundreds of different lures. It would take several lifetimes to become expert in all fishing methods and to learn the details and peculiarities of each type of lure.

As in any other type of activity, the real expert specializes in a few types of fishing and concentrates on a limited number of lures. When I first began salmon fishing I tried everything. I used spoons, wobblers, plugs, herring strip, whole herring, minnows, flies — you name it.

When I began to specialize, I began to catch more fish. For my own purposes and in the areas I fish, I have found that herring strip works best for chinooks and bucktail flies work best for coho, especially in late season. When fishing chinooks, I fish almost entirely with herring strip. If I see some jumping coho or blueback (small coho) I will troll a bucktail fly down the middle.

As the summer progresses and coho begin to arrive in greater numbers, I use both herring strip and bucktail flies. In September and October I find that bucktails produce the most coho and the most spectacular fishing.

Compared with previous years, however, salmon are now more scarce and running deeper, so I am changing my preference. I still prefer bait (minnows, herring, anchovies, and strip) for chinook salmon, especially near spawning areas. For feeding chinooks, I find that our "Picture Perfect" photographic lures work for both chinooks and coho under most circumstances. Hoochy and flasher are most effective for pink and sockeye (and coho in some situations), but flashers tend to spoil some of the fun of playing a fish.

Many fishermen find it hard to specialize when they see other anglers taking fish on lures they do not have in their tackle box. They will rush home and buy those lures for the next trip. As a result,

they soon have every lure in the tackle store and they don't know how to use any of them.

If you see a fish taken on a lure different from your own, try to learn how you can apply your own gear to the situation. Since size and color are important for inducing a fish to strike, you can try to match the size and possibly the color of the successful lure.

FINDING THE FISH

The next task is to get our lure where the fish are feeding.

Back eddies

These circular currents of water are caused when the water comes around a point or other obstruction and circles back behind it.

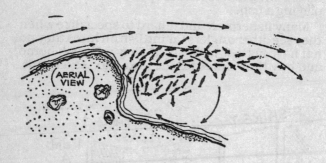

Herring and other bait fish gather in these back eddies and attract feeding salmon. The accepted way to fish eddies is to run down with the tide and circle around through the back eddy. This allows you to cover the water thoroughly and quickly. If you try to go against the current, you may find it difficult to cover all the water. The fish will most likely be found just along the edge between the current and the back eddy.

Remember that the back eddy is on one side of the point on the flooding tide and on the other side on an ebbing tide. Many fishermen will fish without success at the same spot they previously caught salmon when the fish may be only a few hundred feet away on the other side of the point.

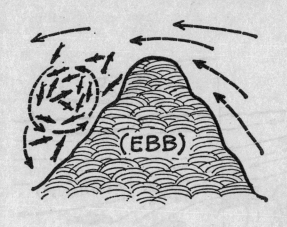

(AERIAL VIEWS)

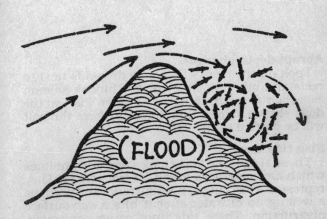

(CURRENT)

Abrupt depth changes

Look on the charts for sharp drop-offs next to reefs and other shallow areas. Chinook salmon especially frequent this type of water. Fish on the downstream side of this drop-off where the bait will be carried to the fish.

Fish tide lines

These are the obvious ripples and current lines which are sometimes found far from shore. They represent a merging of tidal currents and perhaps a welling up of water after it hits a sub-surface obstruction. These tide lines cause concentrations of bait and fish, especially coho.

Find sea birds

Feeding coho can be found almost anywhere and feeding marine birds are the best tip for finding them. These birds are often feeding on bait fish which have been forced to the surface by hungry coho. Washington State Department of Fisheries officials have made observations on the relative value of various birds as indications of feeding salmon.

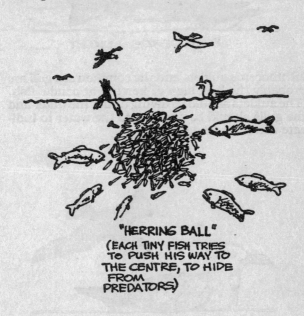

"HERRING BALL"
(EACH TINY FISH TRIES
TO PUSH HIS WAY TO
THE CENTRE, TO HIDE
FROM
PREDATORS)

RHINOCEROS AUKLET

● Rhinoceros auklets and the common sea gull are probably the best sign of herring or candle fish. (The auklets should be diving under the water and the gulls should be diving into the water to indicate active feeding.)

SEAGULL

● The small Bonaparte gull may be feeding on small bait fish but might also be feeding on plankton.
● Grebes or cormorants alone are not a good sign of feeding salmon.

STAYING WITH A
FEEDING SCHOOL OF FISH

When I was a charter fishing guide, I had to produce salmon every day. My customers didn't really care how many fish we caught yesterday or about the big run due next week. They wanted to catch fish today.

When I was out on the water almost every day, it was relatively easy to stay with schools of feeding fish. I would go where they were yesterday and start with the lures and depth that had been successful then.

In the course of this daily fishing, I discovered an important clue which told me when the main concentration of fish had moved. On certain days, we would start catching runt fish, a lot smaller or thinner than the fish we had caught previously. We would also sometimes catch fish with an old wound, usually a badly torn mouth or deformed jaw.

This invariably meant that the main school had moved. These weaker fish couldn't compete for food with the healthier fish, so they were stragglers, feeding in areas just behind the main school and taking the left-overs, so to speak.

When this happened, I would begin to search out the main school again before I lost it completely.

MIGRATING FISH

When salmon begin to migrate toward their spawning river, studies show that they move close to shore, often in shallow water. One theory suggests that they are following the same route by which they went to sea as fingerlings and instinctively follow the same route back. They will move along close to shore for quite a distance then sometimes rest and feed. This close-to-shore pattern starts right near the open sea hundreds of miles from the spawning river (at the entrance to the Strait of Juan de Fuca, for example).

For fall chinook salmon these migrations can

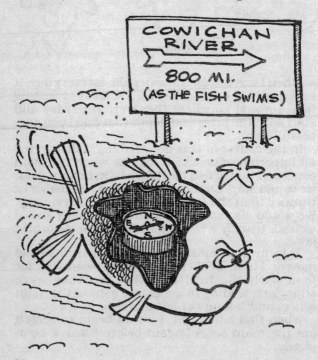

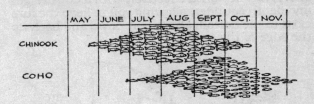

	MAY	JUNE	JULY	AUG.	SEPT.	OCT.	NOV.

CHINOOK

COHO

start as early as May, but most are underway by about the second week in July and carry on into September. For coho they start in August in most areas and carry on into October and even November. These maturing fish represent most of the sport catch during the summer and fall months. So it is important to remember:

Many fishermen wander around all over the bay or fishing area while a few top fishermen stick right up against the shore and catch most of the fish.

Some fishermen complain that they are afraid of snagging on the bottom, or afraid of reefs or kelp beds. These are all possible hazards, but a good chart or some local knowledge, plus common sense, should allow you to get right in close to shore without any problem.

This close-in fishing is not only more productive, but more fun as well since the salmon are in shallow water and it takes less weight to reach them. And when I say close to shore, I mean really close.

In most areas, you should be close enough to cast a spinning lure to the shore. In deeply shelving areas, you can get much closer, sometimes within 20 or 30 feet of the water's edge.

These same suggestions apply when fishing

kelp beds and shallow reefs off-shore.

Some steeply shelving drop-offs (inshore or off-shore) can be fished effectively with a downrigger and depth sounder, allowing you to keep the lure close to the bottom all the way down and back up the edge of the reef.

Drift fishermen often concentrate where back eddies and drop-offs meet. This type of location is often a "hot-spot", where fish school regularly. Major points of land with cliff-like shorelines or narrow passes have sharp drop-offs and fast currents and eddies where migrating salmon will congregate.

Drift fishing, either mooching or Buzz Bomb jigging, is often deadly in this situation. The angler can position his boat in exactly the right spot, say on the edge of the drop-off and on the tide line, to keep his lure almost continuously within the range of fish below. (Further information on the increasingly popular driftfishing is in Heritage House book, *Driftfishing — The British Columbia Way*).

FISH CLOSE TO SHORE!

KEEP A DIARY

Department of Fisheries records over many years indicate that salmon migration patterns are extremely consistent. The big runs of chinooks and cohos tend to pass the same points of land

MISS JONES... LOOK UP CONDITIONS ON JULY 11, 1902, AT 4:27 A.M....

and arrive near the spawning rivers at almost the same date each year.

This is consistent with the habit patterns of other animals. The great fur seals return to the Pribilof Islands off Alaska to mate and raise their young at approximately the same date each year. The swallows and other birds migrate back to their nesting grounds on a precise annual schedule.

In some areas such as the Strait of Juan de Fuca, many different runs are mixing as they come through the area. Since the size of each run will vary from year to year, it may appear that the runs are changing their migration time. Upon close examination, however, we find that this is not true.

What is really happening is that each varies in size every year. A large Fraser River run might pass Sooke or Port Angeles in late August each year while a Skagit river run has an opposite ten-

A THEORETICAL EXAMPLE:

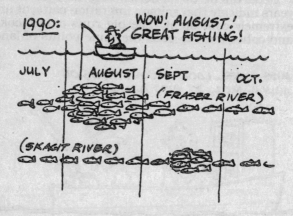

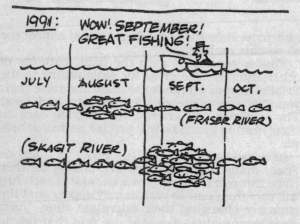

dency, it may appear that the main run was in August one year and September the next.

This migration timing becomes more obvious as you get near the river mouth. The chinook runs arrive in mid-August at Cowichan Bay every year and the cohos show up in mid-October. While the size of the run may vary, the timing changes very little.

For this reason it is wise to keep a record of each fish you catch. This will give you valuable tips on where to fish next year at the same time.

FISHING DEPTH

One of the biggest reasons for failure of experienced fishermen is not fishing at the correct depth. You might be in the right spot at the right time, but your lure is above or below the feeding fish. Listed below are some general rules for determining fishing depth.

●Coho are generally found at depths of 30 feet or less. Canadian government troll fishing experiments off Vancouver Island turned up coho from 30 to 60 feet but most at 30 feet. Washington State Fisheries sport experts state that coho are usually found in the top 30 feet of water.

● Feeding chinook salmon (before they start on their spawning migrations) are often found in 60 to 90 feet of water. Canadian government tests turned up most chinooks at 90 feet. Washington experiments found 60 to 70 feet deep to be most effective for chinooks.

●Fish shallow (from right on the surface to 15 feet) when you see feeding birds working herring or candle fish.

- Chinooks are often right on the surface at the crack of dawn and near dusk.
- An excellent spot for shallow fishing is right up against the shore.

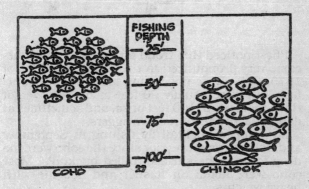

The above depth figures still apply in areas off the West Coast of Vancouver Island and in the northern part of Georgia Strait. However, both coho and chinook seem to be running deeper off the south end of Vancouver Island. (See following page.)

ARE SALMON GOING DEEPER?

My own experience, and that of many anglers, indicates that both coho and chinook are moving deeper each year.

I first noticed this trend about 1973 and it became very pronounced in the summer and fall of 1975. Coho were not taking lures near the surface, but were usually 60 feet or deeper. We got them regularly at 100 feet or so, and sometimes at depths of 150 feet on downriggers.

My favorite bucktail fly fishing in September and October was very poor since the coho were too deep to grab the surface trolled bucktails. Most coho were taken on flasher and hoochie with heavy weights.

We were experimenting with new downrigger techniques at this time. We found the "normal" depth to be at least 100 feet, but often they were much deeper. It was quite common to find schools of immature feeding chinook (two to seven pounds) at 160 to 180 feet. During late September we found them schooled at over 200 feet for weeks on end.

No one knows why the salmon are deeper, but

my theory is that it is related to heavy fishing pressure, especially from commercial seiners and gillnetters. Commercial nets have become so efficient that they form an almost impenetrable barrier to the migrating salmon. The fish that escape tend to be those which swim very deep and go under the solid rows of nets.

If only the deep running fish survive to reach the spawning grounds, then it is logical that their offspring will also tend to run deep. The age old law of nature — survival of the fittest — gives future generations the characteristics that allowed their ancestors to complete their life cycle.

It is frightening to think where this trend may go. If the fish go deeper, the nets will follow them down. After a few salmon life cycles, the fish could be so deep that sportsmen will be unable to get them, even with downriggers. We can only hope

that recent trends are temporary and that the salmon will again move to shallow water. Meanwhile, downriggers are an excellent means of getting down to the fish, while still allowing you to play them on light tackle.

GETTING DEEP

Many fishermen dislike using wire lines and heavy weights to get down deep and subsequently have poor fishing success. But there are a number of ways to have good sport while fishing deep.

Use light line: A thin diameter line creates much less friction in the water — 20 pound test line is adequate for catching salmon up to 50 or 60 pounds if they are properly handled. Even 15 pound test line is satisfactory for most fishing. When buying line, take a close look at the diameter. Some types of 20 pound test lines are much thinner than other brands.

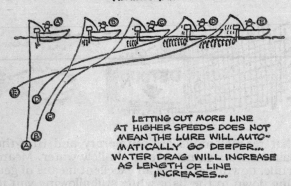

AS BOAT TROLLS FASTER, WATER DRAG OVERCOMES WEIGHT OF LINE & LURE, PULLING IT TOWARDS HORIZONTAL...

LETTING OUT MORE LINE AT HIGHER SPEEDS DOES NOT MEAN THE LURE WILL AUTO-MATICALLY GO DEEPER... WATER DRAG WILL INCREASE AS LENGTH OF LINE INCREASES...

Troll slowly: The slower the boat, the steeper the angle of line. (If you stop completely, the line will go straight down providing there is no tide or wind action.) The major problem here is that many lures will not work properly at very slow speeds.

Whole herring, cut plugs, strip and spinners can often be made to work very well at slow speeds. Certain wobblers and lure types will also work well.

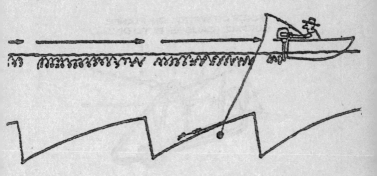

Put the motor in and out of gear: This technique not only allows you to get down deep, but also allows you to fish several different depths and at the same time can add special action to your lure. Put the motor in neutral and let the line sink until it either just touches bottom or reaches an angle of 75 degrees from the horizontal. Then put the motor in gear and the lure will gradually work its way up to normal trolling angle. You will often get a strike while the lure is fluttering down or just after the motor is put back in gear.

Use trip weights: There are a number of gadgets on the market which allow you to use any heavy weight (tin cans full of concrete, plastic bags full of rocks, or pieces of scrap iron) which are dropped when the fish strike. Big John makes a downrigger release which can also be used to hold the drop weights mentioned above.

Planers: These rectangular planing surfaces are rigged so that the force of water passing over them causes the planer to dive, pulling the line with it.

Planer

FORCE OF WATER ON PLANER
SURFACE CAUSES IT TO DIVE...

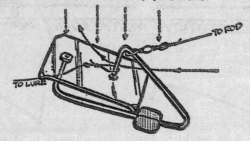

TO ROD

TO LURE

PULL OF FISH CAUSES PLANING
SURFACE TO DROP; SWIVEL
SLIDES DOWN, RELIEVING
FORCE OF WATER...

The major disadvantage with planers is that they require a very stiff rod to hold the pressure and sometimes will not trip on small fish.

EFFICIENCY OF LEAD WEIGHTS

A pound is a pound in air, but not under water. As we all learned in high school physics, any submerged object loses weight to the extent of the volume of water it displaces. Therefore a dense object (lead) loses less weight under water than one not-so-dense (concrete).

This is the great advantage of lead, by far the most dense of the less expensive metals. Lead is far more efficient as a sinker than iron for example. Concrete is another favorite lead substitute, but it loses fully half its weight under water. Part of this loss can be overcome by using iron filings or chunks of iron in place of sand or gravel in the mix.

Another disadvantage of substitute materials is their increased friction when trolling. Some anglers have placed rocks in an old sock or plastic bag and used this as a weight, only to find that friction drag pulled the line back at such an angle that much of the potential depth was lost. If you plan to use disposable weights, ones which fall off after every strike, an inexpensive weight is important. For downrigger fishing, where the weight is retrieved on a separate line, lead weights are certainly worth the extra money.

Speaking of friction, the most efficient weight is a sphere or round ball. This encloses the maximum weight in the least surface area and creates the minimum drag. Fancy streamlined weights, especially for downriggers, cost a lot more money, but actually give less depth per pound.

DOWNRIGGERS

This has become a fairly popular method of fishing deep with light tackle. A few Pacific coast sportsmen have rigged up home-made versions of this gear, but the technique has been greatly refined in the Lake Michigan area.

This is the location of the extremely successful introduction of West Coast coho salmon a while back. Coho eggs were transplanted and hatched for release into Lake Michigan. The coho have flourished (see chapter on fishing the Great Lakes) and developed a whole new multi-million dollar sportfishery. Thousands of new motel rooms, marinas, restaurants, tackle shops, etc. have sprung up to serve the thousands of new

salmon fishing enthusiasts.

Coho are often a surface feeding fish, but hot summer weather and warm surface water tend to drive them into the depths of the lake at certain times. Downriggers were developed in the Great Lakes area to take the fish during these periods.

This device is simple in concept. A separate wire line hooked to a large reel and short stiff rod supports a heavy weight. A light fishing line (with its own rod and reel) is attached near the weight, and a tripping device allows it to pull free when a fish strikes.

This leaves the weight hanging on the downrigger while the fisherman plays his fish with no weight at all. The downrigger weight is retrieved separately. Many models are equipped with footage counters which measure the amount of wire wound off the reel. This allows the fisherman to calculate the exact depth he is fishing at all times.

This type of precison depth fishing has proven very effective in the Pacific Northwest. With a good chart, an experienced boatsman can troll

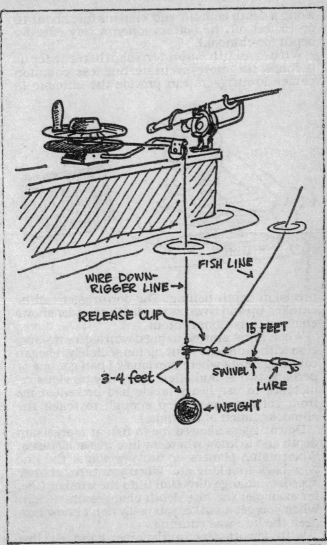

WIRE DOWN-
RIGGER LINE →

FISH LINE

RELEASE CLIP

15 FEET

3-4 feet

SWIVEL ↑

LURE

← WEIGHT

along a depth contour and keep his lure about 10 or 15 feet off the bottom (often a very effective depth for chinook).

With a depth sounder (depth recorder is perhaps the more accurate but less common name) downriggers can provide the ultimate in

precision depth fishing. The downrigger can be cranked up and down as the depth sounder shows changes in bottom contour.

When I first started using downriggers my success with chinooks went up immediately. I began catching limits where previously I had got one or perhaps two — and often none. (My previous reluctance to use heavy tackle had prevented me from getting down deep enough to reach the chinooks much of the time.)

Downriggers allowed me to fish at a precision depth and to know where my lure was at all times. When using planers or heavy weights, the line goes back in a long arc. When you turn, change speed, or change direction (into the wind or tide, for example) the lure depth changes drastically. When you get a strike, you really don't know how deep the lure was running.

With downriggers, on the other hand, the line

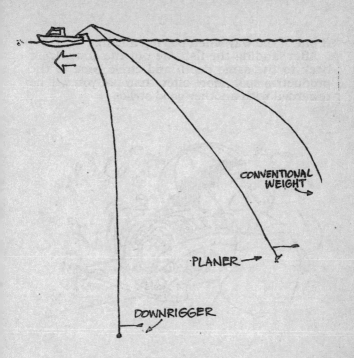

CONVENTIONAL WEIGHT

PLANER →

DOWNRIGGER

goes down at a much steeper angle (I use a 10-pound weight), and changing speeds does not affect depth as much.

goes practically straight down (I use a 10-pound weight) and changing speeds or water conditions have little effect on the depth.

The knowledge of lure depth is the key to catching chinooks (or coho when they are down) once you locate them. The fish are often at a precise depth and you need to get the lure back to this same depth to make a big catch.

When you get a strike on the downrigger, note the depth on the counter before retrieving it (to get it out of the way when playing a fish).

After landing the fish, we put the downrigger back to the same depth and circle back to the productive spot. More often than not you will be rewarded with another good strike.

My major problem with these early Great Lakes downriggers was a continuing battle against corrosion. To overcome these problems, I contacted Scott Plastics in Victoria who have long experience in designing fishing tackle to help develop a downrigger suitable for West Coast sea fishing. The Scotty downrigger has become the best selling unit on the West Coast with its stainless steel and corrosion resistant parts. (Almost all downriggers, however, are now designed to resist salt water corrosion).

There are many sizes and models of downriggers ranging from lake troller models for freshwater fishing to heavy duty extension arm models for fishing from large deep-sea fishing boats. Electric downriggers are becoming more popu-

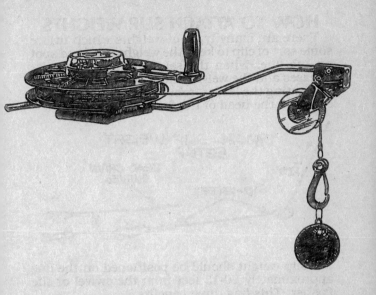

lar, although for reasons known only to Federal Fisheries and Oceans, prior to 1993 they were illegal for sports use except by special permit.

Editor's Note: Ottawa bureaucrats have been waffling for four years over whether or not to make downriggers legal in B.C. As noted above and on page 153, they were supposed to be legal in 1993 but were not. By 1994, however, the incredible dithering with its corresponding waste of taxpayers' money may be over and depthsounders may be legal—but check the regulations!

HOW TO ATTACH SLIP WEIGHTS

There are many types of weights which utilize some sort of clip to keep the weight at a fixed spot on the line. When the salmon strikes, the clip releases and the weight slides down to the swivel separating the leader from the main line or to the swivel at the head of the flasher.

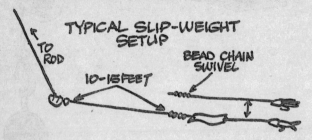

TYPICAL SLIP-WEIGHT SETUP

TO ROD

10-15 FEET

BEAD CHAIN SWIVEL

A slip weight should be positioned on the line approximately 10-15 feet from the swivel or the flasher. This has three benefits:

● The weight is far enough from the lure or flasher so that it does not interfere with its action.
● The weight is far enough away so that the salmon will not be distracted by it.
● When weeds or other debris are picked up by the line, they will slide down and be stopped by the weight, before they get close enough to the swivel or lure to foul it or scare away the fish.

TO ROD (AFTER TRIPPING)
PEETZ
TO LURE→
(BEFORE TRIPPING)

Ivan Peetz, manufacturer of the widely used Peetz weight, recommends that the clip on the weight be positioned toward the lure rather than toward the rod. It will work with the clip facing either direction, but can be tripped more easily by the fish when the clip faces the lure.

Some fishermen put the clip toward the rod so they can reel right up to the rod tip where the force of the weight bumping the rod tip trips it. This allows them to reel in the last 15 feet of line. In my opinion, this can be hard on the rod tip. It is just as easy to reach out and jerk the line when the weight is close to the boat. This accomplishes the same thing.

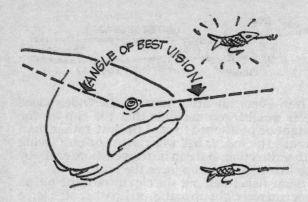

LURE DEPTH

When you are trying to decide how deep to put your line, you should remember some basic facts about light conditions and about the anatomy of a salmon.

The eyes of a salmon are toward the top of its head which makes it far easier for it to see up than down. Since all light under water comes from the surface, it is far easier for a salmon to see a lure looking up against the light where it is outlined clearly than in looking down.

For this reason it is better to have the lure slightly too shallow rather than too deep.

TROLLING PATTERNS

Three lines seem to be the optimum number for most sport fishing boats. In order to keep lines from tangling it is a good idea to have the center line at a radically different depth from the two side lines. (Unless, of course, you are trolling three bucktail flies right on the surface. These are easier to keep from tangling.) The two preferred depth patterns are as follows:

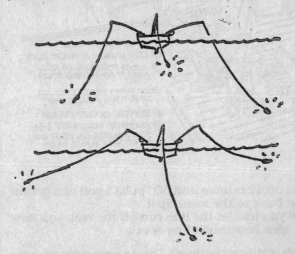

If you feel that the fish are most likely to be deep, use the trolling pattern with two deep lines and vice versa if the fish tend to be shallow.

When using downriggers, additional trolling patterns are possible because the lines are pulled almost straight down and tangling is less likely.

Here are some additional suggestions for trolling:

When you start fishing: put each line at a different depth. When you get a strike, put other lines at the same depth.

If you are not getting any strikes, change weights and depths every 15 minutes until you get a strike. Keep track of the amount of line out by counting the "pulls" of 18 inches or so. If you get a

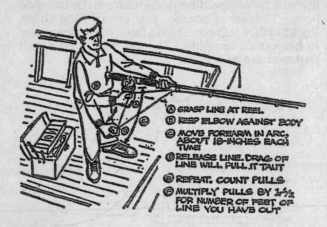

(A) GRASP LINE AT REEL

(B) KEEP ELBOW AGAINST BODY

(C) MOVE FOREARM IN ARC, ABOUT 18-INCHES EACH TIME

(D) RELEASE LINE. DRAG OF LINE WILL PULL IT TAUT

(E) REPEAT. COUNT PULLS

(F) MULTIPLY PULLS BY 1½ FOR NUMBER OF FEET OF LINE YOU HAVE OUT

fish on 12 ounces and 50 "pulls", you can get the line back to the same spot.

If you just let the line run off the reel, you have no idea how much line is out.

Fish a zig-zag pattern: This is especially effective in working along a tide rip or current. Changing direction gives the lure extra action, causes it to change depth and exposes it to fish which may be lying on either side of the tide rip.

Zig-zag fishing can also give clues on fishing speed and depth. If you get strikes on the inside line on a turn (when the lure slows and sinks) it may mean you should fish slower and/or deeper.

If the strike is on the outside line (the lure may speed up and become shallow) it may indicate a faster troll or less weight.

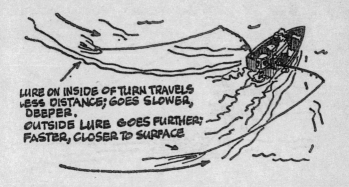

LURE ON INSIDE OF TURN TRAVELS LESS DISTANCE; GOES SLOWER, DEEPER.
OUTSIDE LURE GOES FURTHER; FASTER, CLOSER TO SURFACE

Vary the speed: Sometimes the fish will bite only if your speed is right. If you get strikes when pulling in your line, go faster. (If they strike when letting out, go slower and/or deeper.)

Coho seem to prefer a fast moving and erratic lure. Flatfish and some herring baits can be made to spin and twist extremely rapidly and often the coho prefer this. They also seem to prefer a bait moving fast through the water. Some coho fly experts troll almost at planing speeds.

Vary the length of line: This is often critical when fishing flies or other fast lures right on the surface. Actively feeding coho often strike best when the fly or spoon is only 20 to 30 feet from the boat. I have had coho grab a fly or herring strip right beside the boat when putting the lure in the water to check the action.

One theory suggests that the coho are attracted by the propeller wash (they think it is a milling school of feed) and they don't see the lure if it is too far from the boat.

On the other hand, coho sometimes won't touch a lure, especially a fly, unless it is 150 feet from the boat. This seems particularly true as they approach their spawning river.

Stay with the fish: Feeding fish are often concentrated in a small area. When you catch a fish, see a fish caught, or see jumping fish, by all means fish intensively in this area. Inexperienced fishermen will often stumble on a school of feeding fish and catch a nice one. Then they will wander all over the place and wonder why they don't catch more. The expert will quickly mark the spot when he gets a strike and come back to that same spot as soon as the fish is landed. He will work that tight area over and over again to find other feeding fish in the same school.

If you run into a school of feeding coho away

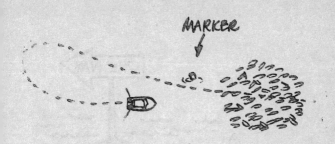

MARKER

from shore or in some area not easily marked, you can throw over any floating object to mark the spot. Some people throw over a seat cushion, boat bumper, even an empty bottle (although these should be recovered later). These floating objects will move slowly with the tide and are effective in marking a school of feeding fish.

Fish in one direction: Sometimes you will notice that all strikes come when you are fishing in one direction. When this happens, don't waste time

fishing back the other way (often against the tide or wind). Pull in your tackle, run back and fish in the productive direction. After covering the section where they are biting, pull up and repeat the process.

Fish hard when "the bite" is on: Salmon usually feed actively only once or twice a day. These feeding times seldom last more than 45 minutes to an hour. This is obviously the time to keep your gear working, but it is surprising what many anglers will do just when "the bite" gets underway. They will catch a nice fish, then spend half an hour admiring it, taking pictures, celebrating with a drink, or stopping for lunch with their tackle on board the boat. When they finally start fishing again, "the bite" is all over.

Check your lure frequently: Pull in your line and check it every 15 minutes or so. A bit of weed, an unseen strike, a fouled hook, or many other things can ruin the action and you have no chance to get a fish. This pulling in and letting out also lets you test various speeds and depths as the lures come in and out.

IMPORTANCE OF A GOOD HELMSMAN

Trolling for salmon is a team effort. A poor helmsman at the wheel can negate the best efforts of the other anglers on board.

Top producers fish with a definite trolling plan. They know that certain "hot spots" (in back ed-

dies, over feed concentrations, abrupt depth changes, etc.) provide most of the strikes. So they spend as much time as possible trolling through this productive water.

This is not as simple as it sounds. Getting into position for a good pass through the "fishy" spot may involve considerable maneuvering. If a sharp drop-off is involved, you must approach it just right or you'll leave your gear decorating the reef.

Wind, tide and other boats in the area can also hamper your efforts to get set for another run over the fish concentration.

Plan your turns to take advantage of wind and tide so you can get back into position quickly.

Turning the wrong way can put the boat so far away from the fish that it can take 20 to 30 minutes to get back to the hot spot. (If I am forced into this position, I will often pull in the lines and run back.)

When fishing with a less experienced partner, it is usual for the veteran to rig and work the fishing tackle while the tyro handles the steering. By all means tell him your fishing plan and give him steering instructions.

I used to have some very frustrating trips with beginners who spent 95 per cent of the trip over unproductive water. Then I realized it was my own fault for not telling my helmsman what I wanted.

I suspect that this is one of the big reasons for fishing arguments between husband and wife. These lovely ladies (who probably weren't too keen to go in the first place) are told to steer while expert husband handles the tackle.

He does a slow burn while she steers aimlessly around the bay. How does she know if he doesn't tell her? Eventually, the boat passes over a reef or into a mass of floating debris and pent-up emotions explode in a flurry of accusations and harsh words.

ASK OTHER FISHERMEN

One of the quickest ways to find the right depth, the right bait and the right trolling speed is to ask other fishermen in the same area. When I first arrive at a fishing spot, I make it a practice to troll near the other boats and ask them how they are doing. Most fishermen are proud to tell you about their catch.

After congratulating them on their success, I then ask the following questions:

● "Where did you catch it?" (I try to find out exactly what part of the area.)

● "How deep were you fishing?" (I try to get an answer in terms of length and weights used.)

● "What lure were you using?" (I also try to find out whether or not a flasher was used, etc.)

● I usually do not ask about trolling speed but just watch the boat and pace myself beside it.

It is surprising how many fishermen will watch one boat pull in fish after fish and never be curious enough to find out how he is doing it. Not one in a hundred fishermen will refuse this information if asked in a friendly manner.

BEST TIME TO FISH

Salmon are such unpredictable creatures that they can bite at any time of the day. However, it is generally agreed that:

● The first two hours after daybreak are often very productive. Both chinooks and coho are often right at the surface and feeding actively at the first

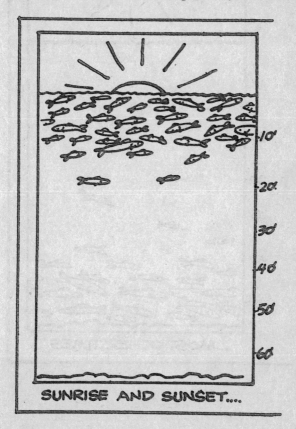

SUNRISE AND SUNSET....

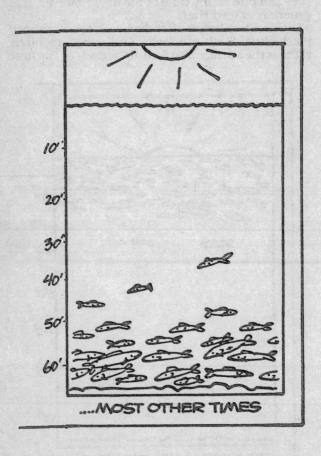

....MOST OTHER TIMES

crack of daylight. (During the summer months, this means being out on the water as early as 4 a.m. to be ready for the early bite.) When the sunlight hits the water, it often signals the end of the bite as the fish move deeper.

● Slack water. Fish will often start to bite about an hour before slack water and feed off and on until about an hour after slack water. This seems especially true regarding chinooks.

● Tidal rips and currents. Whenever these rips are formed by changing tidal action can be a good time for cohos to bite.

● Late evening. Chinook salmon often feed in the late evening. I have often watched the great majority of sport fishermen give up without success and start home from the fishing grounds just as the sun is setting. One or two experienced fishermen will stay on and catch several good chinooks between sunset and total darkness. I have often landed my last fish by flashlight.

● When a travelling run of coho first arrive at a new spot they sometimes feed very actively. They can often be caught all day long with a more intense bite coming about slack tide.

EFFECT OF WEATHER CONDITIONS

Troll fishing experiments by officials of the Washington State Department of Fisheries indicate that the following tips have some merit.

● Clouds, fog, or rain will sometimes mean that the morning bite will last longer.

● Wind conditions will not have any effect on the fishing except to make it uncomfortable in rough water.

● Muddy water caused by run off from storms or melting snow can hurt fishing because visibility is much reduced.

● Chinook salmon do not seem to bite well when bright sunshine is on the water.

My own personal experience has been that coho bite as well, or better, on bright sunny days as on cloudy days. (I think the reason is that they can see the lure better.)

MUDDY FRESH-WATER LAYER

Muddy water, perhaps a thin layer of fresh water floating on salt water can often mean there will be good catches of salmon in the clear water under this mucky layer.

One clue that the layer is thin is to watch for clear water pushed up into the wake of your boat by the propeller.

Washington State Fisheries experiments also indicated that feeding habits varied drastically from one spot to another. In some areas, the fish would bite near slack tide (which comes at a different time each day) while in other areas they found that the fish would bite at the same time of day regardless of the condition of the tide. (Now you can see why I stated at the beginning of the book that fish were ornery creatures and there were no hard and fast rules.)

WINTER FISHING

It is a shame that so many fishermen put away their boats and fishing tackle shortly after Labour Day and miss the exciting winter fishing available in protected areas.

Winter fishing is primarily for immature chinooks since cohos are only 12 to 15 inches long in the winter. Winter chinooks are actively feeding fish and very sporting to catch. They are usually found in 40 to 90 feet of water and right on the bottom. A good way to catch these fish is to let out the line until it hits bottom and pull up 5 or 6 feet to get above the cod and other bottom dwellers.

Since winter fish are often feeding on large mature herring, large baits are very effective. They bite best in the early morning and near tide changes. Washington State officials found that there was not much of an evening bite, but I know several local fishermen who do very well in late afternoon.

Downriggers are very effective in winter fishing, giving the depth control necessary to get to the bottom dwelling chinooks.

SPAWNING FISH NEAR RIVER MOUTHS

This is a special kind of fishing where most of the normal rules are thrown right out the window.

These fish will strike lures and bait under certain conditions but they do not seem to be feeding. Examination of the stomachs of fish caught near river mouths invariably shows the stomach to be completely empty.

Some people feel that fish strike out of anger or irritation while others say that, while not actively chasing feed, they will strike out of instinct at bait passing close to them.

Coho seem to prefer a very fast troll and can be taken on large bucktail flies, spoons, plugs, and herring baits. They will often feed right at the surface for the first hour or two after daylight and then go down.

Chinooks usually bite best at the crack of dawn and late evening.

A depth-sounder survey at Cowichan Bay on Vancouver Island early one October turned up some very interesting results. Coho could be seen jumping and finning on the surface and most fishermen would have assumed that was the place to fish. However, the depth sounder revealed that the great mass of fish was located 40 to 45 feet down. (An analysis of coho catches at about this time showed that most fish were taken on herring baits trolled at about this depth.)

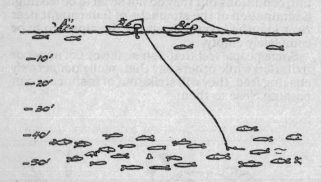

Washington State results tended to confirm this. They found that best fishing was at 40 feet even when substantial numbers of fish were seen jumping on the surface.

As the fall season wears on, coho feeding habits keep changing. After about October 15, coho will

more actively attack such lures as orange Flatfish with black spots (many orange lures with black spots seem to become more effective about this time), Buzz Bombs, Deadly Dick's, and various other spinning lures. The large Flatfish is usually trolled, but Buzz Bombs and other spinners are most often cast out and let sink to 40 or 50 feet. They are then retrieved in a pattern shown which allows the lure to flutter down periodically during the retrieve. Most strikes occur during the "flutter down" action.

DOGFISH SHARKS

These small sharks travel in great schools which can spell trouble and frustration for most sport fishermen. Their razor sharp teeth can nip through almost any leader resulting in the loss of some expensive lures.

Here are some thoughts about dogfish:

● The presence of dogfish does not mean an absence of salmon in the area. I have seen fishermen pack up their tackle in disgust and move off after hooking one or more dogfish. They are often feeding on the same herring or minnows as a big school of salmon and it is just a matter of catching the salmon instead of the dogfish.

PHOOEY! ALL DOGFISH!

● Because of the shape of its body and underslung jaws, the dogfish attacks a bait with an awkward, head snapping bite. This clumsy action coupled with its poor eyesight makes it difficult for him to catch any but a relatively slow moving bait. *Trol-*

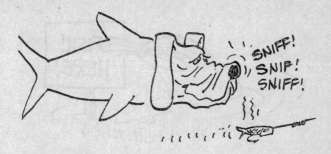

SNIFF! SNIP! SNIFF!

ling a bit faster will often keep them from catching the bait.

● Dogfish have an extremely acute sense of smell and are much more discriminatory in favor of natural baits. Switching to artificial lures will often attract salmon and put off the dogfish.

● Be extremely careful when handling hooked dogfish. It is advisable to gaff them over the side and hold them there while you give them a sharp blow between the eyes. (Of course, it's not necessary to kill dogfish, you can release them!) Then you can extract your hook and lure. If the hook is deeply imbedded, it is probably better to cut off the hook and replace it.

Be extremely careful of the sharp teeth and watch for the writhing tail and spiked dorsal fins.

But don't throw your dogfish away. As pointed out in Heritage House book. *How to Cook Your Catch*, they are excellent table fish if handled properly and under 24 inches. (Larger ones have a high mercury content.)

My avid gardener wife has asked me to save the dogfish carcasses for fertilizer. I cut each dogfish into three or four pieces and put one chunk under each tomato plant. The growth rate is amazing! Another good use for dogfish is as prawn bait. Commercial prawn fishermen find that dogfish are the best bait if the traps are set for more than two days. (Herring is best for short sets.)

SEALS AND KILLER WHALES

Do seals and killer whales scare away the salmon? Many anglers are convinced that they do. Since both are predators which feed on many marine fish including salmon, they reason that salmon will avoid areas where they are present.

This seems logical, but my own observations indicate that, with one notable exception, it is not true. Indeed, since seals usually hang around where there is something for them to eat (usually where there are baitfish, bottomfish, and very often, salmon), I find them to be a positive sign when looking for salmon.

I'm sure that salmon avoid seals, but "out-of-sight-out of mind" seems to be the salmon's behavior pattern. They are very often present in the same area with single seals or colonies of seals. I assume that they will run from a pursuing seal, then resume normal feeding activity when he is gone.

Killer whales seem to have the same effect on feeding salmon — especially coho. I can remember several occasions (in Active Pass, off East Point, off James Island) when coho and killer whales inhabited the same areas. We played two coho simultaneously off East Point one sunny summer afternoon while a huge pod of about 40 killer whales snorted and splashed on all sides of the boat.

The notable exception is in a river estuary or other areas where salmon are gathering for their spawning run. The presence of killer whales in this situation apparently strikes terror into every salmon in the area. In the regulated area at Rivers Inlet where every salmon catch must be registered, fisheries department records show that catches of 50 big tyee a day drops to zero for 24 to 36 hours after marauding whales move through. Similar dropoffs have been noted in Cowichan Bay and other pre-spawning areas.

Seals and sea lion populations

Now that new conservation regulations protect seal and sea lion populations, they are becoming bolder with sport fishermen. They have learned that a hooked salmon is easy to catch and they steal them right off the fishing lines. They tend to select a successful angler and follow his boat for hours at a time.

I lost a nice salmon to a fat harbour seal one evening and moved a quarter of a mile away to try fishing another area. No sooner had we begun trolling than the same seal popped up behind our boat, even though there were 30 or 40 boats in the area. He had chosen us to catch his dinner for him!

MOOCHING

Mooching is driftfishing with natural bait and light sinkers. The boat drifts slowly and allows the bait to work with tidal action. This method of fishing is rapidly replacing trolling in many areas and is often the most productive way to fish. (Heritage House book, *Driftfishing: The British Columbia Way*, contains detailed instructions on all forms of mooching.)

BASIC MOOCHING HOOKUPS

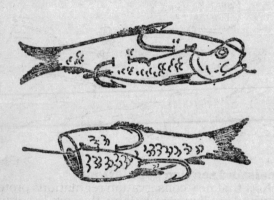

For chinook use a 15 pound test leader and for coho or small feeding chinooks, use 10 pound leader. The leader should be about one foot shorter than the rod—but not less than five feet.

Your bait must revolve to catch fish — slow spin for chinooks, fast spin for coho.

When fishing, let out the line at a controlled speed to give an angle of 40 to 60 degrees from the horizontal (assuming tidal action). If water depth is less than 90 feet, it is a good idea to let out the line right to the bottom, then retrieve slowly to find the depth of the feeding fish.

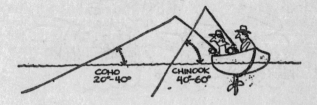

When fishing coho, let the line out at an angle of 20 to 40 degrees from the horizontal to a depth of 20 to 30 feet and then retrieve slowly. Coho mooching is most effective along tide rips and currents.

When the fish strikes, feed line as it will usually move off a short distance and then stop. When it starts to run again, strike hard.

The majority of strikes will come when the line is being let out. This is especially true with chinooks.

Mooching is a most pleasant way to fish. You can fish with the motor shut off and enjoy the quiet surroundings. You can also fish with very light tackle and get a lot of sport out of playing the fish. You can also fish more people per boat than when trolling.

SOCKEYE SALMON

Both commercial and sport fishermen are becoming adept at catching sockeye salmon on hook and line. These prime quality fish, with brilliant red flesh, were formerly taken only in gillnets and purse seines.

Hoochy, Flashtail and other squid or shrimp-like lures are most effective for catching sockeye in salt water. Fish them behind a flasher or dodger with 20-pound monofilament and 18-32 inches of leader, with 28-29 inches the most favourable.

Dead slow is the most effective speed. You might even try drifting or putting the engine in and out of gear. Since sockeye are often down deep, slow trolling also helps you get down where they are feeding.

Since sockeye feed primarily on planktonic organisms and shrimp and squid-like creatures, a wildly darting lure (such as those used for herring feeders) is not as effective. The best color seems to be pinkish red in the sea, but fresh water anglers, especially on Lake Washington near Seattle, have found that bright red, orange, and pink are the killers. Small plugs and spoons with a steady wiggling motion are also very effective.

In Canada, sport fishing for sockeye in non-tidal waters is forbidden, so the fresh water suggestions apply only to angling in U.S. waters.

Sockeye are notorious for schooling at a precise depth. So unless your lure is within a narrow depth range, your chances at sockeye are slim. Be very careful in counting line pulls so you know the amount of line out at all times.

Better still, use a downrigger for precision depth fishing. (See section on "Downriggers".)

WHAT TO DO WHEN YOU
GET A STRIKE

After all our careful preparation, skillful handling of the lure, and finding the salmon, we will finally achieve a major goal. We will actually get a salmon strike.

A strike can come in many forms.

A screamer: This type of strike comes from a coho (or sometimes a chinook) which grabs the lure and takes off like a shot. This causes the rod (in the rod holder) to arch back sharply and the reel to start spinning out rapidly. This type of strike oc-

curs most often when fishing with bucktail flies or other lures using light weights. The fish has little resistance to overcome, so his initial high speed run is transmitted directly to the rod and reel.

A series of sharp jerks: Depending on the fish and the type of tackle, this type of strike can be followed by a screaming reel. When using heavier weights and flasher or dodgers, the initial strike of the fish is often absorbed by this tackle and the effect on the rod is a series of sharp jerks.

If you are trolling slowly, the fish will sometimes

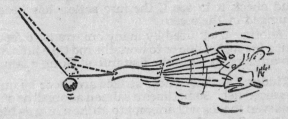

grab the lure and then simply shake his head in an attempt to dislodge the hook. This is often followed by a screaming reel when the fish realizes it cannot shake free.

A "touch": This type of strike is indicated by a short, sharp bend of the rod tip which immediately returns to normal position. This usually indicates that a salmon has nipped at the bait or brushed against it but is not hooked. If the fish does not return for another strike within a minute

" TAG--YOU'RE 'IT'!! "

TOUCH!

or so, it is probably a good idea to bring in your line and check it to see if the lure action has been changed by the strike.

Another trick used by many anglers is to feed out a few feet of line or to work the rod tip a little in an attempt to tease the fish into striking again.

"Tiddler" strikes: These strikes are those by undersized fish. Sometimes a salmon as small as six or seven inches will attempt to strike a lure as big as it is. When these small fish hit your lure, you may not even see it if fishing with heavy weights or flashers. This is another reason for checking your line frequently to be sure you are not dragging a tiny salmon around all day.

If fishing with flies, spoons or other small lures with light weights, an undersized fish will make the rod bend in a series of rapid vibrations causing the tip to "dance".

Downrigger Strike: On smaller downriggers, the strike is seen first on the downrigger, not the fishing rod. The wire and pulley begin jiggling as

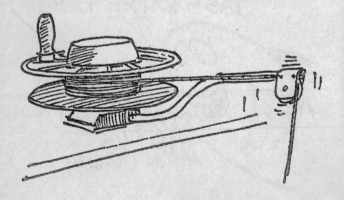

the salmon pulls to free the release pin.

On heavier duty models, the downrigger is quite rigid, and the first sign of the strike is often the rod popping loose, going slack momentarily then the reel singing — the salmon is on the line with no weight at all. It will usually head for the surface (you might have to wind furiously to keep up with it) and put up a spectacular fight right on top.

WHAT TO DO AFTER THE STRIKE

I have watched some anglers keep right on trolling after they get a strike. They pick up the rod and "horse" in the fish, over-coming not only the pulling of the fish but also the friction and resistance of the line and gear being pulled through the water by the moving boat.

This tactic might be alright for commercial fishermen, but in my opinion, it is very undesirable for sport fishermen. Not only does it destroy the thrill of feeling and playing the fish, but the risk of losing the fish is greatly increased by the extra strains of the moving boat. A much better way to proceed is as follows:

Put the engine in neutral or turn it off altogether. This will stop the boat and give you a freely drifting platform from which to play the fish. It also stops the propeller which could otherwise cut the line when the fish is close to the boat.

If fishing in a crowded area, it is often advisable to move out away from the other boats before putting the engine in neutral. This gives you lots of room to play the fish without danger of tangling with other lines. It also allows the other boats to troll into the productive area where you just got your strikes. Very courteous and sportsmanlike.

Pull the rod from the rodholder and set the hook if necessary. A salmon will usually set the hook itself in the process of striking the lure. This is especially true in fast trolling and in light tackle fishing. It may be necessary to set the hook on a light strike (as already noted, indicated by a series of short jerks) but this should only be a short jerk of the rod butt to set the hook past the barb.

If the line goes slack after the strike or while you are playing the fish you should reel rapidly until you can again feel the fish. Some people are so concerned about pulling too hard that they will allow the line to go slack (especially if the fish

starts swimming toward the boat) and will have no idea where the fish is or what it is doing.

Reel in the other lines: A hooked salmon dashing frantically around the boat can easily wrap the line around other trolling lines, causing a terrible snarl. It destroys the fun of playing the fish since it is now pulling against the other line as well as your

own. You also have no control over the fish and it can pull free by pulling sharply against the other line.

If you leave the other lines in the water, they will also drop down vertically, possibly hanging up your lure on the bottom.

The best bet is to have the other fishermen reel in their lines as quickly as possible and store them out of the way.

Get the net ready: Many fishermen keep their landing net stored in the forward cabin or under a pile of lifejackets or other gear. (Maybe this is because they seldom if ever use it.) Many people also keep their landing net in its folded or collapsed position for easy storage.

After the other lines have been reeled in, one of the fishermen should get the net and prepare to land the fish. I have seen nets torn and lunch boxes and other gear strewn all over a boat in a frantic attempt to get the net just as the salmon is alongside the boat.

Clear the cockpit: Move any unnecessary gear out of the area where you will be landing the fish.

Tackle boxes, thermos bottles, extra clothing, and other gear should be stowed out of the way so that the person handling the net will not trip or slip on them at a crucial moment. We once lost a large salmon when the net handler stepped on a soft drink bottle and fell against the fishermen just as the salmon made a last minute lunge under the boat.

PLAYING A SALMON

Remember two things and you won't lose many fish:

Keep the rod up. Brace the base of the rod against your body and grasp it above the reel. (Don't hold it below the reel or you'll have no leverage.)

Hold the base of the rod up at least a 45 degree angle. The tip will, of course, be bent down toward the fish, but the bending rod will give you lots of "shock absorber" action to cushion sudden runs and jerks by the salmon.

If you lower the rod and point it toward the fish,

it is pulling directly against the reel. A sudden jerk and the hook can easily tear out or the line break.

"Let him run." More fish are lost by trying to hold the fish too tight than by playing it too loose. When the fish tries to run, let it go. This is the real excitement of fishing. The screaming ratchet is the most exciting sound in the world.

If you are using a "knuckle-duster" reel, get your hand off the reel handle instantly when the fish starts to run. Put your hand on the back edge of the reel to provide a gentle braking action if necessary.

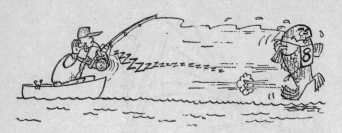

Do not try to wind the reel backwards to let out line. The fish will almost certainly jerk the handle from your fingers and the knobs will fly around and smash you hard on the knuckles. This sudden bang can also snap the line.

I never cease to wonder why people insist on holding fish so tight. It is so much better to let them run.

You should attempt to keep the line from going slack, but this is usually not difficult. Since gills are a most inefficient breathing apparatus (they are forced shut when the fish swims rapidly) the salmon will have to stop to breathe before he runs far.

NETTING THE FISH

The net should be a proper salmon net with a long enough handle to put the entire net comfortably in the water from the deck of a boat.

The fish should be brought to the net rather than you chasing the fish around the boat. When the fish is properly played out, you can lead him over the net head first, then lift the net around him.

Other comments on netting include these:

• Hold a played-out fish (it should be lying on its side) with its head just breaking the surface of the water. Do not lift its head or a substantial portion of its weight out of the water, as this can cause the hooks to tear out and you will lose your fish.

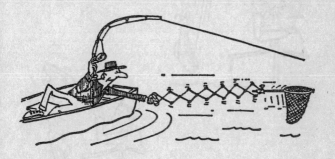

• Be very careful not to let the fish brush against the net before you are ready to land it. If you are using a multiple hook set up, a dangling hook can catch into the net and allow the fish to jerk free.

• Do not try to net the fish tail first. A powerful flip of the tail against the net and the fish can leap free. The force of this jerk can often break the line or tear the hook out.

• If the fish jumps in close to the boat, lower your rod tip immediately. Otherwise the line will come tight before the fish hits the water and can jerk the

119

hooks out or break the line.

- If the fish dives beneath the boat, plunge the rod tip down so that it can swim under the boat without fouling on the boat bottom or propeller. You can then work the rod around the stern of the boat until the line is clear.
- When lifting a fish into the boat, raise the net at an angle to minimize strain on the net handle.

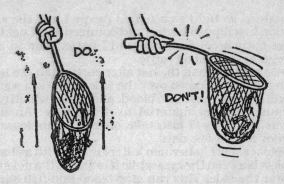

DO!

DON'T!

●Many anglers hold the bottom of the net against the handle as they prepare to net a fish. This keeps the bag of the net from hanging in the water where the fish may bump it. Others tie a line to the bottom of the net and pull the net tight against the handle for the same purpose.

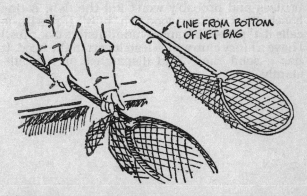

LINE FROM BOTTOM OF NET BAG

This system works well for many anglers, but I tried it once and abandoned it. With my hands tight on the handle and intent on landing a large chinook, I found it difficult to release the line holding the net bag. As a result, the netting remained as tight as a tennis racquet and the salmon just flipped his tail and bounced out. Luckily, we got a second chance and I netted him in my regular "loose-bag" style.

● Be sure to wash the net after each catch. Swishing it up and down over the side in the sea water will remove the slime, blood, and scales which can cause the net material to deteriorate. An unwashed net will also take on a very unpleasant odor after a few days.

● Most expert fishermen kill their fish with a sharp blow between the eyes while it is still in the net and over the side. This can stop blood and fish slime from getting all over the boat. Moreover, the fish will not have time to thrash around in the net and lose his scales. It will be a much better looking fish to take home.

Be sure to hit the fish between the eyes. This will kill him surely and cleanly. If you hit it further back, you will spoil some excellent flesh with blood bruises and probably won't kill the fish. A tiny baseball bat makes a good fish "billy". (Rhys Davis calls it a "priest" because it administers last rites.) I have a fancy club with a lead insert in the head. It has a solid "heft" and dispatches all fish efficiently.

EXAMINE STOMACH CONTENTS

One of the most important things you can do after catching a salmon (or even a cod or rockfish) is to open its body cavity and examine the contents of the stomach. This fish may have been "triggered" to strike your lure and the preferred feed could be entirely different.

These stomach contents can give important clues as to the feeding habits of the fish. The size, shape, and color of the preferred feed should be examined closely. If the fish have been feeding on herring or candlefish it is relatively easy to imitate the size and shape of this feed with either natural bait or spoons, Flashtails, Twinkle Skirts, or other similar lures. If the salmon has been feeding on baby shrimp or other planktonic organisms, it is impossible to duplicate the size and shape of this feed with any lure large enough to hold a hook. Coho especially are fond of this type of feed in the spring and fall. This is when many fishermen say that the coho are "fussy" or "they won't bite on anything".

This however, is the time to attempt to imitate

WHAT — NO WINE SAUCE?

the color instead of the size and shape of the natural feed. These tiny shrimp and planktonic organisms often have a slight pink or grey color. (You have to remember that the color of the feed will bleach out in the strong digestive juices of the stomach. Once you identify the type of feed, you can use colors imitating that feed when it is alive and fresh.)

These are the times when bucktail flies, hoochies, octopus, flash flies and similar lures are extremely effective. These lures come in many colors and you can likely get one to match the color of the feed. These lures also have a fluttering tail action which many feel imitates the swimming action of small shrimp and other plankton.

There are also some small plastic and metal spoons with colored stripes which can be effective under these circumstances.

KEEPING THE FISH FRESH

Keep the fish out of the sun. Ideally they should be kept in an insulated box surrounded by ice or artificial ice packs.

Fish will keep quite well if covered with a damp cloth or burlap sack. Even wet newspaper can help a great deal. Water should be sprinkled on the cloth or paper to keep it moist.

Fish should be cleaned as soon as possible. Smaller fish are especially prone to going soft if not cleaned or kept quite cool.

SPRINKLE COLD SEA WATER TO KEEP BURLAP COOL

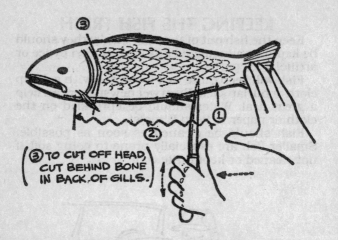

3 TO CUT OFF HEAD, CUT BEHIND BONE IN BACK OF GILLS.

CLEANING SALMON

Salmon are easy fish to clean. Simply insert a knife blade into the anal vent and slice the thin layer of meat up the belly to a point approximately under the eyes.

Cut out the gills by cutting off the connecting points at the roof of the mouth and on the bottom jaw.

You then grasp the esophagus and strip the entrails clean.

Next slit the protective skin covering the large clot of blood along the back bone. This can then be scraped out easily with a spoon.

The fish should then be rinsed lightly in cold water to remove leftover blood, then wiped dry with a cloth or paper towel.

This is called a "showclean" since the fish still has his head and tail. It's great for "showing" the fish to family and friends back home.

Cutting off the head and tail can make cleaning somewhat easier and requires less storage space. (Be sure to save the heads, tails and entrails for crab bait.)

FILLETING

Fish fillets are an excellent form for barbecuing, smoking, or pan frying. Fillets are easy to handle, have no major bones and are easy and compact to store in the refrigerator.

To fillet the salmon, start with a very sharp knife. Insert the knife from the top along the back until you feel the edge of the knife touch the backbone, then work the blade along the backbone and against the bones rising vertically in the back of the fish. Insert the knife in the lower part of the tail and work forward from the tail and from the backbone down, keeping the knife blade against the bones forming the rib cage. The final cut is along the side of the fish in the back of the gill to free the fillet. This process is repeated for the other side of the fish.

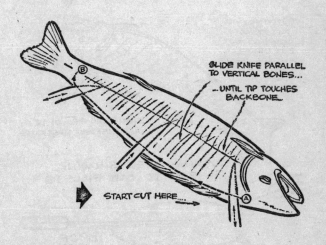

SLIDE KNIFE PARALLEL TO VERTICAL BONES...

...UNTIL TIP TOUCHES BACKBONE.

START CUT HERE....

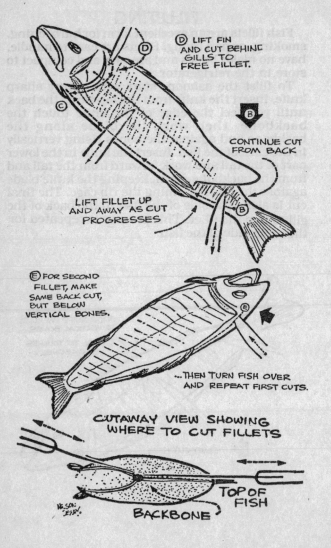

D LIFT FIN AND CUT BEHIND GILLS TO FREE FILLET.

B

CONTINUE CUT FROM BACK

LIFT FILLET UP AND AWAY AS CUT PROGRESSES

E FOR SECOND FILLET, MAKE SAME BACK CUT, BUT BELOW VERTICAL BONES.

...THEN TURN FISH OVER AND REPEAT FIRST CUTS.

CUTAWAY VIEW SHOWING WHERE TO CUT FILLETS

TOP OF FISH

BACKBONE

PRESERVING THE CATCH

Salmon taste best when eaten as fresh as possible. However, salmon also keep relatively well when processed.

Canned salmon is excellent, but home canning should be done carefully according to established practice, pressure cooking the fish 90 minutes at 15 lbs. pressure. (The correct procedure is spelled out in detail in many authorative home-canning cookbooks.)

Frozen salmon may deteriorate in flavor and texture if not properly wrapped or frozen in water. However, it should keep well for several months under optimum conditions.

Smoking or kippering salmon is growing rapidly in popularity. Hot smoking adds tasty flavor and will preserve the fish for several weeks under refrigeration. There are a number of small home smokers on the market which are easy to use and turn out a good product.

THE GREAT LAKES

by Darryl Choronzey

ABOUT THE GUEST AUTHOR

Darryl Choronzey has been a fishing fanatic since boyhood. As a youth he grew up near the Great Lakes and had ample opportunity to pursue his favorite sport on rivers and lakes throughout Ontario, and in several neighboring American states.

He has followed and been involved with Great Lakes salmon programs since their inception, and has assisted the Ontario Ministry of Natural Resources on many annual egg taking operations.

Darryl's reputation as an expert fisherman and authority on Great Lakes salmon and trout led to his appointment as co-ordinator of the "Toronto Star Great Salmon Hunt", the world's richest fishing derby.

Darryl Choronzey is publisher and editor of *Ontario Fisherman Magazine*, and author of *Ontario Steelhead Fishing*.

DIFFERENT TECHNIQUES

After experiencing the Great Lakes salmon fishery from its inception, and spending several seasons on West Coast waters from Oregon to Alaska, I am unable to state which region offers the most spectacular salmon fishing. What can be noted though, is the distinct differences by which anglers from the Great Lakes area go about catching their fish compared to their counterparts along the Pacific northwest coast.

Pacific anglers must take into account the effects of tides, currents, baitfish schools and other conditions peculiar to ocean fishing, while Great Lakes anglers are more concerned with water temperature, depth and lure color — in other words, factors more distinctive to a freshwater fishery.

Both groups may be successful in their own back yards, but would probably need adjustment periods before succeeding in the others' area. This is not to imply that some West Coast techniques will not work on Great Lakes salmon, or vice versa, for productive anglers are usually those willing to experiment. The answer lies in observing the conditions under which you are fishing, then applying various techniques to match those conditions.

PACIFIC SALMON TRAVEL EAST

Great Lakes coho, chinook and pink salmon can all trace their ancestry back to forbears that thrived in the salt water of the Pacific Ocean. Transferring them from the West Coast was not an easy task, however. Between 1873 to 1933 several attempts to introduce coho and chinook were made. All were unsuccessful.

To understand why these attempts were undertaken one need only refer to history. Completion of the Welland Canal in 1829 dealt a devastating blow to the ecological balance of the Great Lakes through the introduction of sea lampreys. These

parasitic intruders moved upstream from the Atlantic Ocean and slowly spread throughout the large lakes where slow moving lake trout and burbot became easy victims.

As lake trout and burbot populations dwindled their prey fish, alewives and rainbow smelt, became dominant — and problems began to develop. Both species exhibit cyclical die offs. Allowed to increase unchecked these periodic die-offs often reached millions of tons. These high mortality

rates posed serious health threats to communities situated around the Great Lakes, and nearly caused a total collapse of the region's tourist industry.

While the public demanded a solution to the smelt and alewife situation, two Michigan biologists, Dr. Howard Tanner and Dr. Wayne Tody, planned yet another attempt at introduction of Pacific salmon into the Great Lakes.

In 1964 they obtained one million coho eggs from the Oregon State Fish Commission. These eggs were hatched and cared for in their Michigan facilities, then released as 18-month-old smolts in the spring of 1966. From the original one million eggs 850,000 fingerlings survived to be released into Bear Creek and the Platte and Big Huron rivers.

The first indication that the Great Lakes could support Pacific salmon occurred the following autumn when thousands of "jacks" began returning to the rivers of their release. Their growth rate had been truly amazing, for they averaged close to 19

inches in length, and weighed from two to six pounds.

Salmon fever took hold as thousands of fish-starved Great Lakes anglers rushed to greet the returning coho. The following year proved even better, for during the summer of 1967 adult coho began appearing virtually anywhere a lure could be trolled through the water. The size of these fish was also mind-boggling. Typical Lake Michigan adult coho weighed over 12 pounds, and some trophy fish went over 18 pounds. *The Great Lakes salmon fishery had arrived.*

That the work of doctors Tanner and Tody could be termed successful would be an understatement. Many angling experts now rate the Midwest salmon sport fishery as the best in the world — and rightly so. Depending on their location Great Lakes anglers now have the opportunity to fish for trophy-sized coho, chinook and pink salmon. As a back-up fishery, many hatcheries also provide fishing enthusiasts with lake trout, hybrid lake trout, brown trout, Atlantic salmon and steelhead   but Pacific salmon continue to draw the most attention

TIPS FOR SPRING FISHING

Each year finds most Great Lakes salmon anglers praying for an early spring. As snow melts and rivers thaw, inshore lake waters begin to warm. Schools of alewife and smelt move into the shallows to spawn, and hot on their trails follow predatory salmon. During March, April and May, coho caught in such areas may average between

two to six pounds, and chinook may range anywhere from three to 30 pounds.

Match lure to bait. Most experts agree that during the spring it's best to match lure size to that of the baitfish salmon are feeding on. As early-spring forage fish are fairly small it pays to keep the size of offerings to a minimum. Two- to three-inch wobbling plugs or spoons usually outproduce dodger/plug or dodger/spoon combinations during the first months of open water season, so leave the big attractors in the tackle box.

Depth Important. When lake waters warm to about 44 degrees Fahrenheit, alewives and smelt move inshore to spawn. Locate the whereabouts of these forage fish and you will usually find coho and chinook nearby.

It's generally agreed that spring coho are most often found closer to shore than chinook. I've often taken small coho in water as shallow as two feet or less. Chinook, on the other hand, tend to

hold out in deeper water where they can bushwhack schools of forage fish from depths of 10 to 30 feet. This feeding trait is most likely due to the chinooks' sensitivity to surface light.

Short or long line? Fishing for shallow-water coho during early spring is most often a case of flat-lining near the surface. While greedy young coho have been known to pick lures right out of the prop wash within a few feet of the boat, my most consistent catches are made with lures trailed 30 to 200 feet behind.

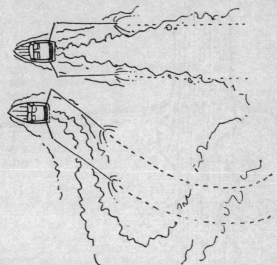

Zig-zag technique. It's a wise coho angler who practises zig-zag trolling patterns while working over the shallows. Lures will be pulled through areas where fish have not been spooked by motor and boat noises, and the zig-zagging movement varies lures speed and action — which may well turn on a hungry coho.

Use planer boards. When coho have been turned off the bite because of excessive boat traffic, or should they happen to be feeding in water too shallow for safe trolling, "planer boards" can be used to take lures well out to the sides of your boat. Planers boards are tethered to the boat by a strong (75- to 200-pound test) line or rope. Lures are trailed behind the planer board by attaching the main line to a mechanical release or elastic band, much the same as a downrigger. A salmon trips the release when it attacks the lure, allowing anglers to fight the fish on light tackle. The use of planer boards for surface-cruising chinook dur-

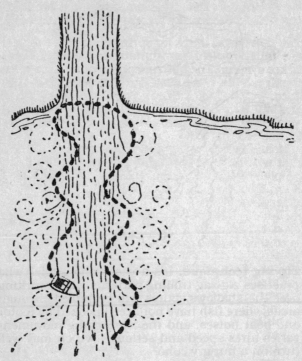

ing early morning and late evening hours can also prove rewarding.

Investigate river mouths: Locate a river mouth flowing into one of the Great Lakes and you have likely found a hot salmon fishing hole. During the spring months river water is often warmer than surrounding lake water. Forage fish are attracted to these warmed areas, as are salmon. I often investigate river mouths for streaks of colored water that reveal the actual discharge point of the river. I then attempt to troll my lure along the mudline (where river and lake waters mingle). Phosphorous (glow-in-the-dark) plugs and spoons often prove lethal in situations where salmon are feeding within the murky waters of a river estuary.

The right lure: Lures for spring coho and chinook are fairly typical throughout the entire Great Lakes system. The hottest coho spoons have been the Krocodile, Little Cleo, Little Jewel, Cop-E-Cat, Loco, Devle Dog, Rattlesnake, Daredevle Klicker and Manistee Wobbler. Keep in mind though, that small spring coho prefer spoons of two to three inches in length.

Most experts using plugs prefer small models that wobble from side to side without diving too deeply. Fire Plug, Tadpolly, Rapala, Bomber, Hot Shot, Kwikfish, Canadian Wiggler and Flatfish all deserve mention.

Chinook anglers often choose much larger lures than those intended for coho, usually ranging from three to six inches in length. An important point to remember is that springtime chinook feed on large baits whenever possible, so choose the size of your lures accordingly.

Overgrown spoons that are all popular for spring chinook are Miller Flutterlite, Manistee Wobbler, Eppinger Flutter Chuck, Northport Nailer, L.G. Johnson, Luhr Jensen Flutterspoon, Westport Nailer, Doctor Hood, Tom Mack, Andy Reeker and Producer.

The most popular plugs with spring chinook anglers are the Luhr Jensen J-plug, Magnum Rapala, Bomber, Dandy Glo, Canadian Plug, Canadian Wiggler, Mac's Squid Plug, and jumbo-sized Kwikfish.

WATER TEMPERATURE MOST IMPORTANT

I am often asked what the most important factor is when it comes to successful Great Lakes salmon fishing. I always reply with the same short and simple answer: *temperature*.

All game and forage fish in the Great Lakes have what I refer to as an *Active Feeding Range* and a *Peak Feeding Temperature*. The Active Feeding Range is the general temperature range at which a particular species can be found seeking food. The Peak Feeding Temperature is the *exact temperature level* where, if all conditions are favorable, a species will most likely be found. It should be understood, of course, that an important factor regarding the Peak Feeding Temperature for either species of salmon is availability of food. If forage

142

fish are not present at that particular level, coho and chinook move about within their Active Feeding Range. This usually means a difference of only a few degrees.

Active Feeding Ranges of coho and chinook overlap those of smelt and alewives, which certainly simplifies matters for salmon anglers. By studying the chart it should be easy to understand why alewives are so attractive to coho and chinook. The Peak Feeding Temperature of coho and alewives is identical, and the one degree of difference between chinook and alewives is negligible in terms of changes in depth.

Species	Peak Feeding Temp.	Active Feeding Range
Coho	54°F	44-58°F
Chinook	53°F	44-58°F
Alewife	54°F	48-72°F
Smelt	50°F	43-56°F

If the magic 53° to 54°F temperature range preferred by chinook and coho is located, that is probably the most productive level at which to fish.

PROBING FOR PROPER TEMPERATURES

You can't locate proper temperature levels without a thermometer. Without a doubt the fastest and most accurate instrument for the job is an electronic temperature probe.

Over the past decade I've depended on a couple of units, a Fish Hawk 520 (Fish Hawk), and a Fish 'N Temp (Lowrance Electronics). Both are capable of sending instant water temperature readings between sensor and indicator by means of a coaxial cable. The only drawback to these units is for accurate readings the boat must be stopped, then the sensor lowered over the side.

A recent model from the Waller Corporation frees anglers from the coaxial cable and time-consuming act of stopping and starting the boat. The sensor is permanently mounted on the down-rigger cable near the cannonball. This provides continuous temperature readings relayed to an indicator mounted in the boat's cockpit.

The folks from Fish Hawk have now introduced the 840 Thermo-Troll. This little wonder allows the fisherman to troll and automatically read both temperature and trolling speed at two depths — on the surface and at the downrigger's cannonball. Believe it or not, there's almost always a difference in current between the surface and at the level the lure is traveling. Knowing the speed of the lure allows an angler to always have plug or spoon swimming with the most enticing sway and wiggle.

WELCOME TO WARMER CLIMES

ELECTRONIC FISH LOCATORS

A "fish finder" isn't necessarily a must item on a Great Lakes salmon trolling boat, but having one aboard definitely goes a long way toward putting more salmon in the cooler by day's end. There are three types to consider:

Flashers. The most economical is the flasher unit. With this type of device the bottom and surface are indicated on the screen by two distinct flashing lights or light bars. If fish pass within range of the unit's electronic impulse they show up as another flashing light between the bottom and surface lights, at a distance corresponding to the depth intercepted. The main drawback with flasher units lies in the fact you must watch the screen at all times in order to see fish moving beneath the boat. Also, many novice anglers find it almost impossible to distinguish between baitfish and salmon.

Graph recorders. The second type of fish finder is the graph recorder, which virtually draws a continuous picture of the bottom and surface, along with everything in between. My advice, based on experience, is if you can afford one, investigate the possibilities, pick out a good one, then buy it. Graph recorders may not give you the same opportunity to meet salmon "almost in person" as does Charlie White's underwater camera, but they are a marked improvement over flasher units.

I prefer the X16 graph recorder over any other unit currently on the sports-fishing market. This tiny little computer marks down the exact location of fish that pass within range of my boat, and produces a permanent record that is often kept on file should I plan to fish the same area another day.

CRT recorder. The third type of fish-finder is the cathode ray tube (CRT) recorder, which resembles a small television set. It works on basically the same principal as a graph recorder, but does not require graph paper. These units are cheaper to operate than graph recorders, but do not provide a permanent record for those, like myself, who like to have them on hand for future reference.

FISH AMONG THE BAITFISH

Once your graph recorder is operating satisfactorily it's wise to look not only for salmon, but also for the baitfish they feed on. In most cases a salmon or other large fish is indicated on the graph paper as a well-defined, inverted "V". Baitfish schools may show up as blotches, cloud-like markings or, depending on the size and density of the school, large inverted "V" shapes. (The ability to distinguish between large fish and baitfish schools comes with practice.)

The important thing to remember is that if you discover the proper temperature, then locate baitfish within the Active Feeding Range of salmon — *stay with the bait*. Salmon have to eat, so if they are not present at the time, they will probably show up before long.

I *always* attempt to run my downrigger cannonball and trailing lure directly through a school of baitfish. They are sometimes so dense that salmon feeding within their mass are not pinpointed by the graph recorder.

Chinook often sulk on the bottom to avoid brightly sunlit water, but may charge upward to strike a flashing spoon or plug as it is drawn through a school of baitfish. It probably represents an injured baitfish, thus an easy meal.

A FRUSTRATING SCENE

With the aid of a good graph recorder you can often witness a chinook or coho stalking your trolled lure. Sometimes this *fishy* behavior can drive an angler crazy with anticipation and frustration. Here is a tip to hasten the strike: Slightly opening up the throttle often adds just enough increase in lure action and speed that the salmon, possibly believing it's been discovered, makes its last, fatal mistake.

Note from Charlie White: Since the last edition of this book, LCD's — Liquid Crystal Displays — have become very popular indeed. These units use hundreds of tiny "pixels" to form a picture of the water from top to bottom. They are similar to a graph or video recorder in showing a profile of the water depth, including the surface, the bottom, and schools of bait fish and salmon. The better quality units have more pixels and therefore show greater definition.

(A big advantage of this type of unit is the fact that it shows up well in bright sunlight as opposed to video recorders which tend to "wash-out". A good video unit will show more detail, but the advantage of LCD's is their lower price.)

A COLOR FOR EVERY DEPTH

One of the most obvious differences I have noticed between West Coast and Great Lakes salmon techniques is that Mid-west anglers are much more flamboyant where lures are concerned. Pacific anglers usually attempt to match their lure to the bait that salmon are feeding on, which accounts for the popularity of silver spoons and plugs of pearl pink, both of which resemble

needlefish, anchovy and herring. Great Lakes salmon anglers differ greatly from this match-the-bait concept, preferring lures and flies in some of the gaudiest colors imaginable.

Color is a reflection of light, and water absorbs light. It does not do so evenly, though, so some colors remain more visible at various depths than others. Thus, color should be matched to the depth being fished.

Winning colours. From the first days of the Great Lakes salmon invasion fluorescent-red Fire Plugs and Flatfish were proven winners with anglers. These wobbling plugs certainly have excellent action, but there was another reason for their prowess. During those initial years downriggers were virtually unheard of, and most trolling was done near the surface. Red, a "soft color", along with orange and yellow, is easily distinguished near the surface by salmon. As they go deeper, though, these colors change: red to black, orange to brown, and yellow to pale white. For deep trolling (45 feet or more) you will probably have more luck with lures of green, blue or chartreuse. Unlike red, orange and yellow they retain their color and visibility.

Match lure and dodger. I often find it important to match my lure color with that of a dodger if I am using one of these attractors to draw in the salmon. I believe that a spoon, fly or plastic squid should represent an injured fish struggling to follow the main school of baitfish. With this in mind I match red flies with red dodgers, green flies with green dodgers, and so on. I break this rule only in water depths ranging from 60 to 120 feet below the surface.

If salmon are ignoring the matched combination I may switch to a chrome dodger and a different-colored lure. The chrome dodger, to my way of thinking, can represent either a small school of baitfish or salmon, either of which may attract curious coho or chinook.

"GLOW LURES" CATCH SALMON

Phosphorous (glow-in-the-dark) lures are available on the West Coast, but Mid-west salmon anglers seem to rely on them much more than their Pacific cousins.

The first "glow plug" to really catch the attention of Great Lakes salmon buffs was the Luhr Jensen J-plug. It is probably still the top selling salmon plug, for it is hard to argue with success.

Phosphorous-coated lures and dodgers are "charged" by exposure to sunlight for a few moments. When lowered into the water the finish emits a glow that often proves lethal to coho and chinook in deep water, or those found cruising the murky water near river estuaries.

Some chinook anglers have taken to night trolling. Phosphorous-finished lures such as J-plugs. Fire Plugs, Fishbacks, or large spoons have produced excellent results. Lacking sunlight, anglers charge their lures in the beam of a flashlight or camera flash attachment.

DOWNRIGGERS AND PLANERS

Charlie White has given a thorough account of the downrigger and its introduction to the Pacific Coast. But for years those of us in Ontario and the neighboring American states had an advantage over our B.C. counterparts. We could use electric downriggers which were banned in B.C. — except for the handicapped — although commercial fishermen could use power to haul up their lines. Until 1993 when downriggers became legal, B.C. anglers used bicep power to crank in their weights, an inconvenience if more than one downrigger is being used. (With four on my boat I

MY COUSIN...
VISITING FROM
THE WEST
COAST...

tip my hat to the genius who developed the electric downrigger.)

If you can't afford a downrigger then turn to planers such as the Deep Six or Pink Lady. The Luhr Jensen Company has a new planer on the market I have found deadly on the often wary chinook prowling Colpoy Bay, just a few hundred

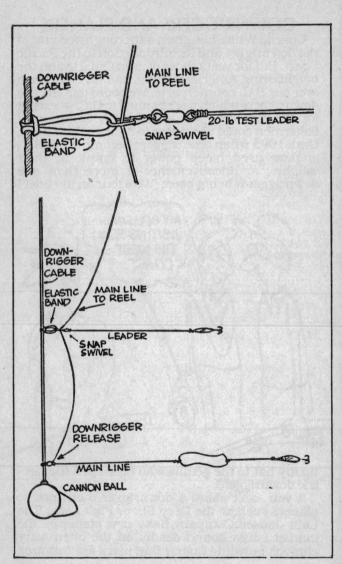

DOWNRIGGER CABLE

MAIN LINE TO REEL

20-lb TEST LEADER

SNAP SWIVEL

ELASTIC BAND

DOWN-RIGGER CABLE

ELASTIC BAND

MAIN LINE TO REEL

LEADER

SNAP SWIVEL

DOWNRIGGER RELEASE

MAIN LINE

CANNON BALL

yards from my back door. Called the Dipsy Diver it dives to the required depth, then planes either left or right, away from the boat. This side-planing ability should definitely add more salmon to your fish box by day's end.

Here's a simple trick that allows an angler using a downrigger to run one or more extra lures on the main line of each fishing outfit. This tactic puts more lures in the water, allowing you more depth coverage for fish that might be at the upper or lower extremes of their Active Feeding Range.

After rigging your main line and lure to the downrigger release, lower the cannonball to whatever depth you wish the second lure to run above the main line. Half hitch a two- to three-inch elastic band to the downrigger cable. Slip a snap swivel over the trailing loop of elastic, then run the main line through the snap before closing it. To the trailing eye of the swivel tie approximately five to eight feet of 20-pound-test monofilament, then attach the lure. (The leader should be no longer than the rod, otherwise netting fish becomes difficult.)

Should a salmon attack the upper lure the elastic band will break. The swivel will then be free to slide down the main line and trigger the downrigger release.

COHO LURES: HOW TO USE THEM

Now that we have learned the basics of where to find salmon and how to get down to them, it's time to look at the choice of Great Lakes lures and how to use them.

New Lures

The tackle business on the Great Lakes has been totally revolutionized by the salmon fishery. It is doubtful that any other region has ever seen so many new lures appear on the market over such a short period of time. All catch fish at one time or another, but like most dedicated anglers I've collected a number of artificials I believe are better than the rest. This is not entirely one person's opinion, though, as many angling acquaintances share my opinion on most of the following choices.

Since coho were the first salmon to be successfully introduced into the Great Lakes, let's look at the lures that turn them on.

Dodger/fly combo

The dodger and fly or squid combination is without a doubt the number one coho producer throughout the Great Lakes. Most experienced anglers allow a distance between dodger and lure of between 8 to 16 inches. The distance from dodger to cannonball release is seldom more than 10 feet. I personally believe the closer the better. If I'm after coho my dodger is often working back and forth less than three feet from the cannonball, and seldom more than five feet. I think coho may be intrigued with the cannonball weight itself and often strike at the lure on the way past.

Matching colors

Remember to match the color of the dodger to that of the squid or fly, then try to determine if it is the proper color for a particular depth. If the color combination fails to interest salmon, continue to

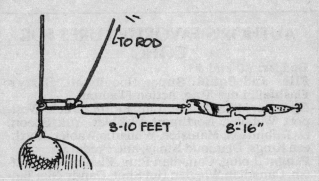

experiment.

I have made no reference to the flasher attractors described by Charlie White as I am unaware of any angler successfully using them on the Great Lakes.

FISH BARE LURES CLOSE-UP

As mentioned earlier, I like my dodger and fly right up tight against the cannonball while fishing for coho. The same holds true while fishing lures bare — without the aid of a dodger.

On a number of occasions I've experimented with a dodger and fly on one downrigger, and a bare plug on the other. Quite often the plug will outfish the dodger/fly combination. This doesn't happen all the time, mind you, but often enough that I usually have one downrigger outfitted with a bare plug, and usually within three to five feet of the cannonball.

AUTHOR'S FAVORITE LURES FOR COHO

Dodger: #0 and #1.
Flies and Squid: Super Hoochytail, Barry's Flashtail, Lure King, Action Flashtail.
Spoons: Miller Flutter Lite, Flutterchuck, Westport Wobbler, Northport Wobbler, Yuk Spoon, L.G. Johnson, Manistee, Williams Wabler, Northern Kings, Diamond Kings, and Predators.
Plugs: J-plug, Canadian Plug, Fishback, Kwikfish, Canadian Wiggler, Hot Shot, Dandy Glo, Tadpolly, Jointed J-plug, Lyman Lure, Sea Bee. cannonball, but don't neglect them for use with dodgers. Because of their side-to-side action lengthen the leader behind the dodger to at least five to 10 feet.

AUTHOR'S FAVORITE LURES FOR CHINOOK

Spoons: Miller Flutter Lite, Flutterchuck, Westport Wobbler, Northport Wobbler, Yuk Spoon, L.G. Johnson, Manistee, Williams Wabler.
Plugs: J-plug, Canadian Plug, Fishback, Kwikfish, Canadian Wiggler, Hot Shot, Dandy Glo, Tadpolly, Jointed J-plug.
Note: Although a few anglers still utilize the dodger/fly combination for chinook, many experienced salmon hunters have found success with spoons and plugs. The key word here is *big*. Chinook are big fish, and if the water temperature is to their liking they will be looking for big baitfish to feed on. Lures should be at least four inches in length, and those of six inches or more won't intimidate full grown chinook salmon.

FALL SALMON ACTION

By late August and early September many adult chinook and coho begin to congregate off the mouths of their natal streams in anticipation of their spawning run. It's during this time, when cooler weather chills the top layer of lake water to the salmon's liking, that small boat (cartopper) operators and shore-bound casters get their whack at the schooling fish.

Trollers often switch from downriggers to top-water tactics with satisfactory results. Although the bright chrome sides of schooling coho and chinook begin to tarnish as their appetites turn from food to sex, head-shaking plugs in three- to five-inch lengths will still entice them (Kwikfish, Tadpolly, Flatfish, Fire Plug, Canadian Wiggler).

Working the mudline, where lake and river waters merge, is often the best bet at this time of year, for salmon often move in and out of the murky river water as their mating urge increases.

SOMETIMES ITS A REAL JUNGLE DOWN HERE...

CASTING FROM PIERS AND SHORE LINES

Hundreds of piers jut out from the shorelines of the Great Lakes. During early autumn anglers situated on these structures can cast at passing salmon cruising as they prepare for their upstream migration.

Most shore and pier casters prefer spoons over plugs or spinners because of their concentrated weight and aerodynamic shape. Depending on the type of rod, reel and line used, the most popular lure weights run from one half to three ounces. Krocodile, Daredevle, Little Cleo, Cop-E-Cat and Little Jewel are all considered excellent choices.

After casting allow the lure to flutter toward bottom before starting the retrieve. Since prespawn salmon are not the voracious feeders of mid-summer, retrieve the lure with just enough speed to provide the desired action.

WHAT ABOUT RIVER SALMON?

I've heard the same statement hundreds of times: "All salmon caught in the rivers are snagged." My answer is "Bull!" This is not to imply that some salmon aren't illegally pulled from rivers, for it is unfortunately true. But a lot more fish are legally taken, and river fishing for salmon can be an exciting and sporting experience.

Enforcement and education will go a long way toward eliminating illegal methods of river fishing, and law-abiding anglers must learn to police their own ranks. The honest majority should not have to suffer because of the misguided actions of a few law-breakers.

When river fishing for salmon the word to remember is "patience." For while those big spawners heading upstream are more concerned with loving than eating, they can be tricked into attacking lures. By continually confronting a salmon with a good-sized wobbling plug you can often aggravate it into walloping the artificial. It may be a case of making a hundred casts, but in the end old man salmon is going to get fed up and put a stop to the nonsense.

I noted the truly aggressive nature of chinook

one afternoon while peering down from a bridge a few miles upriver from Lake Ontario. A school of river chub were feeding in midstream when I spotted a big buck chinook making his way up through the current. Upon spotting the chub he veered away from his set course just enough to scare the living daylights out of the unsuspecting small fry. Now that salmon was definitely not in a feeding mood, so it was probably just a case of being boss of the river. This same aggressiveness holds true when confronted with an overgrown lure, and sooner or later the chinook or coho will get infuriated enough to smack it a dandy clout. Whether it happens on the first or one hundredth cast is what makes river salmon fishing such an interesting challenge.

LIGHT-LINING FOR SALMON

A few years back a Michigan chap, Dick Swan, developed an innovative style of fishing. Tossing aside his "heavy" tackle, Swan began working the rivers with a rod fashioned from a 12-foot automobile aerial of fiberglass. Dubbed a "noodle rod" because of its extreme flexibility, it allowed the use of lines as light as two-pound-test, even against large fish. Such small diameter line allowed for the presentation of small baits in the most natural of manners. With small hooks and single eggs or miniature roe bags, Swan and his growing army of followers began to prove, beyond any shadow of doubt, that salmon would take both natural baits or soft plastic imitations.

Light line tactics are now used by thousands of anglers on Great Lakes tributaries each fall. With the right equipment and a little bit of stealth, even first-time anglers can expect to tie into 15 to 40 pound salmon. Whether they land them, of course, depends on skill and luck — but that's typical of almost all facets of Great Lakes salmon fishing.

*FINI / THE END

Fishing Diary

DATE	TIME	LURE AND COLOR	DEPTH	WEATHER - TIDE	

SPECIES - WEIGHT - WHERE

Fishing Diary

DATE	TIME	LURE AND COLOR	DEPTH	WEATHER - TIDE

SPECIES - WEIGHT - WHERE

Look for these books of outdoor exploration and discovery to help you get the most from B.C.'s great outdoors!

Available at your bookstore or sporting goods store — or you can order them from Heritage House Publishing Company on the convenient order form at the end of this book.

HOW TO CATCH SALMON — BASIC FUNDAMENTALS
by Charles White

This is the most popular salmon fishing book ever written! Here's the basic information you need for successful fishing: trolling patterns, rigging tackle, how to play and net your fish, downriggers — and where to find fish! Also included is valuable Fisheries Department information on the most productive lures, proper depths to fish and salmon habit patterns. This is *the* basic book on salmon fishing in the North Pacific with sales over 120,000. Illustrated throughout.

| 12th printing | 176 pages | $5.95 |

HOW TO CATCH SALMON — ADVANCED TECHNIQUES
by Charles White

The most comprehensive salmon fishing book available! Over 190 pages crammed full with how-to tips and easy-to-follow diagrams to help you catch more salmon. Covers all popular methods — downrigger techniques, mooching, trolling with bait, tricks with spoons and plugs. You'll find tips for river mouth fishing, catching giant tyees, winter fishing, secrets of dodger and flasher fishing, Buzz Bombs, Deadly Dicks, Sneaks and other casting lures — and much more!

| Updated 6th printing | 224 pages | $11.95 |

HOW TO CATCH BOTTOMFISH
by Charles White

While salmon are the "glamour" fish, bottom-fish are tasty and easy to catch. This book shows how to catch cod, sole, perch, snapper, rockfish, and other bottomfish. Best tackle and rigs, baits, when and where to fish. Detailed step-by-step filleting diagrams.

Revised 5th printing   160 pages $5.95

HOW TO CATCH CRABS
by Captain Crabwelle

This book, revised to show the latest crabbing techniques, describes how to catch crabs with traps, scoops, and rings; where and when to set traps; the best baits to use. It includes a detailed description of an easier, improved method of cleaning, cooking and shelling the meat. It's a great book, crammed with everything you need to know about catching crabs.

Updated 11th printing   110 pages $4.95

HOW TO CATCH SHELLFISH
by Charles White

How, when and where to find and catch many forms of tasty shellfish: oysters, clams, shrimp, mussels, limpets. Easiest way to shuck oysters. Best equipment for clamming and shrimping. When not to eat certain shellfish. What to eat and what to discard. A delightful book of useful information. Well illustrated.

Updated 4th printing   144 pages $3.95

HOW TO CATCH STEELHEAD

This book by popular outdoors writer Alec Merriman contains helpful information for novice or expert. Information includes how to "read" the water, proper bait, techniques for fishing clear or murky water, and fly fish for steelhead. Many diagrams and illustrations.

5th printing   112 pages $3.95

HOW TO FISH WITH DODGERS AND FLASHERS

Joined by guest authors Lee Straight, Jack Gaunt and Bruce Colegrave, Jim Gilbert helps you catch more salmon. Find out when to use a dodger or a flasher, all about bait and lure hookups, best lure action, trolling speeds, leader lengths and more.

2nd printing   128 pages $3.95

CHARLIE WHITE'S 101 SALMON FISHING SECRETS
by Charles White

Charlie shares more than a hundred of his special fishing secrets to help improve technique and increase your catch. No fisherman should pass this one up. Illustrated throughout with Nelson Dewey's distinctive cartoons and helpful diagrams.

Updated 3rd printing   144 pages $9.95

DRIFT FISHING

Seven expert Pacific Coast fishermen help you become more productive using Perkin, Buzz-Bomb, Stingsilda, Deadly Dick, and herring. Whether you fish salmon, bottomfish or trout this book of illustrated techniques for mooching, casting and jigging can increase your catch.

Revised 4th edition   160 pages $10.95

HOW TO COOK YOUR CATCH
by Jean Challenger

Tells how to cook on board a boat, at a cabin or campsite. Shortcuts in preparing seafood for cooking, cleaning and filleting. Recipes and methods for preparing delicious meals using simple camp utensils. Special section on exotic seafoods. Illustrated.

8th printing   192 pages $4.95

BUCKTAILS AND HOOCHIES

Trolling bucktail flies is one of the most exciting methods of catching salmon, as well as being very productive. Hoochies have always been the favorite of commercial fishermen and expert Jack Gaunt tells sportsmen how to catch salmon with them.

Updated 5th printing   112 pages $4.95

HOW TO CATCH TROUT

Lee Straight is one of Western Canada's top outdoorsmen. Here he shares many secrets from his own experience and from experts with whom he has fished. Chapters include trolling, casting, ice fishing, best baits and lures, river and lake fishing methods — and much more.

8th printing   144 pages $5.95

AN EXPLORER'S GUIDE TO THE MARINE PARKS OF B.C.
by Peter Chettleburgh

The definitive guide to B.C.'s marine parks. Includes anchorages and onshore facilities, trails, picnic areas and campsites. Profusely illustrated with color and black and white photos, maps and charts, this is essential reading for all yachtsmen and small boat campers.

200 pages $12.95

LIVING OFF THE SEA
by Charles White

Detailed techniques for catching crabs, prawn, shrimp, sole, cod and other bottomfish; oysters, clams and more. How to clean, fillet, shuck — in fact everything you need to know to enjoy the freshest seafood in the world. Black and white photos and lots of helpful diagrams.

Updated 2nd printing   128 pages $7.95

FLY FISH THE TROUT LAKES
with Jack Shaw

Professional outdoor writers describe the author as a man "who can come away regularly with a string when everyone else has been skunked." In this book, he shares over 40 years of studying, raising and photographing all forms of lake insects and the behaviour of fish to them. Written in an easy-to-follow style.

2nd printing   96 pages $7.95

SALMON FISHING BRITISH COLUMBIA:
Volume One — Vancouver Island

Vancouver Island is one of the world's best year-round salmon fishing areas. This comprehensive guide describes popular fishing holes with a map of each and data on gear, best time of year, most productive fishing methods and much more.

128 pages $9.95

SALMON FISHING BRITISH COLUMBIA:
Volume Two — Mainland Coast

Detailed descriptions of nearly 100 fishing holes from Boundary Bay northward to Jervis Inlet, including Active and Porlier Passes, Burrard Inlet, Howe Sound, Gibsons, Lasquiti, Pender Harbour, Egmont and other waters. Information includes where to fish, gear, best lures, location maps and much more.

144 pages $11.95

IN CLOSING — IMPORTANT REMINDER

As noted on page 4, before fishing B.C. tidal waters carefully check the current B.C. Tidal Waters Sport Fishing Guide, published annually by the Federal Department of Fisheries and Oceans. It is available free at sporting goods stores, marinas and similar outlets. The Guide contains all current regulations governing sport fishing not only for salmon but also for halibut, rockfish, crabs, oysters and other species. Check carefully the sections on spot closures which were introduced as a conservation measure to protect not only salmon but also crabs, lingcod and many other species.

BOOK ORDER FORM

Please send me the following books:

...... HOW TO CATCH TROUT .... $ 5.95 .....
...... HOW TO COOK YOUR CATCH .... $ 4.95 .....
...... HOW TO FISH WITH DODGERS
           AND FLASHERS .... $ 3.95 .....
...... LIVING OFF THE SEA .... $ 7.95 .....
...... LOWER MAINLAND BACKROADS:
......   Bridge River Country .... $ 9.95 .....
......   Junction Country: Boston Bar to Clinton .... $ 9.95 .....
......   Thompson - Cariboo .... $ 4.95 .....
...... SALMON FISHING B.C. - Vol 1, Van. Island .. $ 9.95 .....
...... SALMON FISHING B.C. - Vol 2,
......   Mainland Coast — Gulf Islands .... $ 11.95 .....

                              Sub-Total _____
      $1.00 a book postage and handling _____
                               7% GST _____

                                 Total _____

My cheque for $ _____ is enclosed.

**HERITAGE HOUSE
PUBLISHING COMPANY LTD.
Box 1228, Station A
Surrey, B.C. V3S 2B3**

_____
Name (Please print)

_____
Address

_____
City   Province/State   Postal Code

ALL PRICES QUOTED ARE CURRENT AT TIME OF GOING TO PRESS.
AS BOOKS ARE REPRINTED, HOWEVER, PRICES MAY CHANGE.